The *Ars Typographica* Library
General Editor: James Moran

❋✧❋✧❋✧❋✧❋✧❋✧❋✧❋✧❋✧❋✧❋✧❋✧❋

JOHN BASKERVILLE

of Birmingham

Letter-Founder and Printer

❋✧❋✧❋✧❋✧❋✧❋✧❋✧❋✧❋✧❋✧❋✧❋✧❋

Uniform with this Volume
Allen Hutt: *Fournier*
Roy Brewer: *Eric Gill*

Yr most obed.t hble Serv.t
John Baskerville

JOHN
BASKERVILLE

OF BIRMINGHAM

LETTER-FOUNDER

& PRINTER

F. E. PARDOE

LONDON

FREDERICK MULLER LIMITED

1975

First published in Great Britain 1975 by
Frederick Muller Limited London NW2 6LE

Copyright © F. E. Pardoe 1975

Printed and bound by W & J Mackay Limited, Chatham

ISBN 0 584 10354 9

CONTENTS

✳◇✳◇✳◇✳◇✳◇✳◇✳◇✳◇✳◇✳◇✳◇✳◇✳◇✳◇✳

LIST OF ILLUSTRATIONS

✳❖✳❖✳❖✳❖✳❖✳❖✳❖✳❖✳❖✳❖✳❖✳❖✳❖✳❖✳❖✳❖✳

FOREWORD

The first book in this series was devoted to a Frenchman, Pierre-Simon Fournier, who was described, justly, as the "compleat typographer". This book is about an equally great Englishman, John Baskerville of Birmingham, "that enterprising place", who might with justice be described as the "compleat printer" since good printing is not just a matter of operating a press. Baskerville was concerned with everything to do with the art and craft from the design of type to the improvement of the printing press of his day.

Mr. Pardoe urges that it is time that Baskerville was recognised as the greatest printer that England has ever produced, and after reading this work it may be that others will agree. Mr. Pardoe himself has written the greatest book on this extraordinary man—a book which will be used for reference for many years to come, but one which also brings to life the "celebrated typographer" in his gold-laced waistcoat, who had to make his fortune in japanning before he could turn his attention to fine printing. He produced his *Virgil* in April 1757—an astonishing book, as Mr. Pardoe remarks. He wonders whether Baskerville's skill will ever be fully appreciated by twentieth-century minds. If this book even partially assists us to understand the work of Baskerville, the author will have done a great service to the literature of printing. I consider it an honour to have been associated with this work.

JAMES MORAN

ACKNOWLEDGEMENTS

My debts to a number of people who have been generous with their time, expertise and patience are considerable. I must especially mention three: Wm. P. Barlow, John Dreyfus, and C. C. F. Morbey. All three read my typescript and made valuable suggestions for improving it; each drew freely on his own expert knowledge for my benefit and must be given credit for much of whatever merit this work has. They were expert advisers in particular fields, not proof-readers, and any errors in the text are my responsibility alone.

There are others to whom I owe much, particularly the staffs of the libraries I have used: the Birmingham Library, especially Mrs. Ruth Chedgzoy; Birmingham Reference Library, especially Miss Dorothy McCulla and her colleagues in the Local Studies Department; Birmingham University Library; the Bodleian Library, especially Mr. Michael Turner; Oxford University Press, especially the Printer and Mr. Harry Carter; St Bride's, especially Mr. James Mosley.

Acknowledgements must be made to the persons and organisations who have been kind enough to allow me to quote or reproduce material:

The transcription of the letter from Baskerville to the Earl of Bute is taken from a paper by James L. McKelvey in the *Transactions of the Cambridge Bibliographical Society*, Vol. V, pp. 138–41. Thanks are due to the Cambridge University Press for permission to reproduce this transcription.

One letter has been quoted in full, as well as several brief extracts, from Margaret L. Mare and W. H. Quarrel's *Lichtenberg's Visits to England*, by permission of The Clarendon Press, Oxford.

I have quoted a number of brief extracts from *The Letters of William*

Shenstone, edited by Marjorie Williams and published by Blackwell, to whom thanks.

I am especially grateful to the Birmingham Museum and Art Gallery and the Printer to Cambridge University.

I must also thank: Mrs. S. M. T. Stone; Mr. W. O. Duncan; Mr. J. Hunt; Mr. E. C. Martin, whose photographic expertise made it possible for me to show a complete alphabet of Baskerville's type for the first time; and Mr. James Moran, general editor of the *Ars Typographica* series, who has been a constant help.

Finally, I must thank my wife: she corrected the many errors in my first draft, helped to improve it, checked the footnotes, and compiled the index.

INTRODUCTION

It is surprising how little has been written in two hundred years about John Baskerville: the number of books entirely devoted to him or his work can be counted on the fingers of one hand.

It is the more surprising when one looks at his position in the history and development of English printing. If one goes down the list of the great names, from Caxton to Morison, there is no one who can match even the breadth of Baskerville's experience: this man is only a printer, the other only a type-designer, or a type-founder, or a publisher, or a book-designer . . .

Baskerville designed his type; he cast it and set it; he improved the design of the printing-press; he made experiments in paper-making and the use of paper—even if he did not manufacture it; the ink he made was the envy of his contemporaries; he designed the books he printed; he published books; and he printed books for other men to publish. Obviously, he relied on others to help him with some of these things—I am not suggesting that he cast every piece of type himself or that he personally printed every page in every book he produced. But he was, according to William Hutton, of "the true Birmingham model", and that means, among other things, that he was a typical Birmingham "gaffer", capable of doing any job in the factory and usually capable of doing the job better than the man he employs to do it. They are a dying race.

Baskerville was, of course, not an establishment figure; he was, in fact, very much an outsider. He was an innovator, an amateur, a provincial, and he finished his life an agnostic. No wonder that his contemporaries disapproved of him, his type, and his printing, drawing on all their ingenuity to explain why his type was badly designed, his paper not acceptable, or his books not successful. To be fair, it must be pointed out that not all of his contemporaries wrote like that, but many did—and so did some of the nineteenth-century writers. Even Updike, writing in 1922, expressed a fair amount of disapproval. Possibly the best indication of the attitude there has always existed towards Baskerville is the remarkably defensive spirit in which Bennett wrote his book just before the Second World War.

Yet there is no doubt that John Baskerville occupies a unique position in the history of printing. No other English printer made such great contributions in so many ways to the development of the craft, and it is difficult to find a printer from any other country who was as versatile. Printing has always been a craft bound up in its own traditions—technical, aesthetic and social—and innovators have never been popular. Baskerville broke all the rules; but it is surely time that he is recognised for what he was: the greatest printer England has ever produced.

Anyone who sets out to make a study of John Baskerville's life must draw heavily on two books. The first of these is *John Baskerville: A Memoir* by Ralph Straus and Robert K. Dent, published in 1907. The book had its origin in the collection made by Samuel Timmins, a Birmingham antiquarian, who spent the last quarter of the nineteenth century acquiring everything he could which had any relevance to the printer. That collection is now in the Birmingham Reference Library. The book was printed in an edition of only 300 copies.

The other essential book is even rarer. It was a product of the Birmingham School of Printing during the period when Leonard Jay was Head of the School. He regularly produced books and pamphlets—as examples of the work of the School—and he himself edited a collection of Baskerville letters in 1932. Other items of Baskerville interest were also produced and in 1937 there appeared the first volume of a biography of Baskerville written by William Bennett. The second volume came out in 1939. Not even Jay himself was certain how many copies were produced, but just before his retirement he told me, when giving me a copy of the second volume (all the copies of the first volume had long since been distributed) that only a hundred or so had been printed, and that the first volume had been even more limited.

There is a third essential book for any student of Baskerville: Philip Gaskell's *John Baskerville: A Bibliography*, published in 1959 (2nd edition, 1973). This immensely detailed and scholarly work made it completely unnecessary for me to do anything other than to refer to it when any bibliographical matter needed elucidating. This was a considerable relief: even if I had had any bibliographical expertise, I would have been reluctant to set foot in the maze after reading the following passage about Baskerville's *Virgil*:

> . . . uncancelled leaves and cancels, misnumbered pages, and gatherings in different states, appear in so many combinations that it seems impossible to reconstruct a chronological order of printing or issue. It seems likely that a number of corrections were made while the work was in press and that complete volumes were made up of gatherings from different stages of printing . . .

The passage was written by R. D. Townsend and M. Currier on p. 297 of *Papers in Honor of Andrew Keogh* (New Haven. 1938) and has a despairing, even indignant, note about it. It is understandable in people who were trying to sort out the vagaries of Baskerville's printing; it also appears that they had little knowledge of the attitude of mind of an amateur printer using a hand-press and striving for perfection.

I suspect that we are too conditioned by the techniques of the factory printer ever really to understand Baskerville's methods. The concept of make-ready (ensuring that all is right with the type, the machine, the inking and the impression; then switching on the press and the producing of thousands of identical copies with only an occasional, cursory inspection) is one which was impossible before the age of perfectly reliable machinery and mass-production.

In Baskerville's day no two copies of any piece of printing were identical: hand-inking with leather balls and the construction of the press would prevent that. The wonder is that there is so little variation between copies.

The very slowness of the hand-press—the fact that every sheet of paper is taken off by hand, with the chance to look at each impression—means that any printer who is more concerned with perfection than with profit finds it impossible to resist the temptation to look for mistakes, to improve the impression, to change a letter here or a spacing there.

I have used other books than the three mentioned above, but have listed in the bibliography only those mentioned in the footnotes. In order to save space in the notes I have used abbreviations wherever possible, and the bibliography is given in the alphabetical order of the abbreviations rather than of the authors' names. I have also referred to *Aris's Birmingham Gazette* as *Aris*, again to save space. I have used Gaskell's (and occasionally Straus and Dent's) numbering of the ephemera and books throughout.

I

Wolverley is a village and parish about three miles north of Kidder-minster in north Worcestershire. It was here that John Baskerville was born: he was baptised in the parish church, whose register records the fact:

1706: John ye son of John Baskervile, by Sara his wife, was baptised January ye 28.

He must have been born very early in January, or possibly even late in December 1705, for in 1757, writing a letter dated 4th January he says, "I am now advancing apace toward old age being now in my fifty-second year."[1]

According to Thomas Cave, the Baskerville family, spelling their name in a variety of ways, had been resident in the Manor of Wolverley for at least two hundred years, "always influential and of the sturdy yeoman class".[2] The question of where John Baskerville actually was born was the source of a considerable amount of controversy all through the nineteenth century (it was an almost perennial item in *Notes & Queries*), probably due to Derrick who described Baskerville as having been born in Birmingham.[3] There is no doubt that he was born at Sion Hill in the parish of Wolverley, not at Sion Hill House, but at the farm, Upton House, "known latterly as Sion Hill Farm".[4]

John was the last child of his parents, who had many children, most of whom died young. His father was 46 when John was born and Cave

[1] see pp. 43–4 for full text.
[2] Cave: p. 10.
[3] Derrick: p. 2.
[4] *Victoria County History*: Worcs III, p. 567.

suggests that the Sara who was John's mother was his father's second wife. He also suggests that the family came from London though they originated in Herefordshire.[1]

The family were fairly well-to-do and it is interesting to speculate where John went to school. The obvious answer is that he went to Sebright School in Wolverley, but this is not certain as no records exist of the school in the eighteenth century. The school was founded early in the seventeenth century from a legacy left by William Seabright of London, who had been brought up in Wolverley. The impossibility of settling the question of Baskerville's school is regrettable—and not merely for the sake of the completeness of the record: some schoolmaster or writing-master who was teaching in North Worcestershire in the second decade of the eighteenth century must have given Baskerville his "great fondness for print characters" and it would have been pleasant to be able to give him a very belated credit.

There is, in fact, no authentic information about Baskerville between the date of his baptism and 1728 when he was described in a mortgage indenture as "of Birmingham".[2] Various legends have grown up about him. One, that he was a footman at King's Norton (now a suburb of Birmingham; at that time a village outside the town), seems to depend entirely on the memory of the Rev. Mark Noble who said in 1806: "I well remember the celebrated Baskerville, who taught my most respected father to write, and who maintained an acquaintance with him as long as he lived . . ." and in a footnote: "Always inquisitive, I have obtained the following particulars respecting Baskerville. He was a footman, I think, to a clergyman of King's Norton, near Birmingham, who used to make him instruct the poor youths of his parish in writing . . . Leaving this place, he went to Birmingham; there, in a little court or yard near High-town, he taught writing and accounts . . ."[3] Although the *Dictionary of National Biography* describes Noble's writings as "those of an imperfectly educated, vulgar-minded man", it is probable that his account of Baskerville's first few years in Birmingham is substantially correct, though the post as footman seems unlikely in view of Basker-

[1] Cave: pp. 15–16.   [2] see pp. 6–7.
[3] Noble II: pp. 361–2.

ville's family background. Yet John Dreyfus has informed the present writer of a Swedish reference to Baskerville written by Bengt Ferrner who visited the printer in 1760. In it he comments on "his polite behaviour which was the more to admire as he had made his way from a livery servant to considerable prosperity". The reference is from a diary: Bengt Ferrner *Resa i Europa 1758–1762* (pp. 248–9), edited with an introduction by Sten G. Lindberg, published Uppsala 1956. Both Nichols[1] and Hansard[2] give 1726 as the date when Baskerville became a writing-master in Birmingham, and one must assume that he also began to cut gravestones at about the same time.

It is impossible to tell the date of the handsome slate slab preserved in the Birmingham Reference Library, but it must have been cut fairly early in his career as it was obviously intended to act as an advertisement for his services: "Grave Stones Cut in any of the Hands By John Baskervill Writing Master" (he had still not settled on the definitive spelling of his name). From the absence of any signs of fixing holes, it must be assumed that the slab was for display in a shop-window.

There are no known examples of his gravestones extant. In 1818, according to Charles Pye who wrote *A Description of Modern Birmingham . . . in the Summer of 1818*, there were two. Describing the church of St. Mary in Handsworth (then a separate village, now a suburb of Birmingham) he says:

> . . . a humble tomb-stone, remarkable as being one of the last works, cut by his own hand, with his name at the top of it, of that celebrated typographer, Baskerville, but this being neglected by the relations of the deceased, has been mutilated, although the inscription is still perfect, but so overgrown with moss and weeds, that it requires more discrimination than falls to the lot of many passing travellers to discover the situation of this neglected gem. To those who are curious, it will be found close to the wall, immediately under the chancel window . . .[3]

Pye goes on to suggest that this "precious relic of that eminent man"

[1] Nichols: *Lit. Anec.* III, p. 450.   [2] Hansard: p. 310.
[3] pp. 107–8.

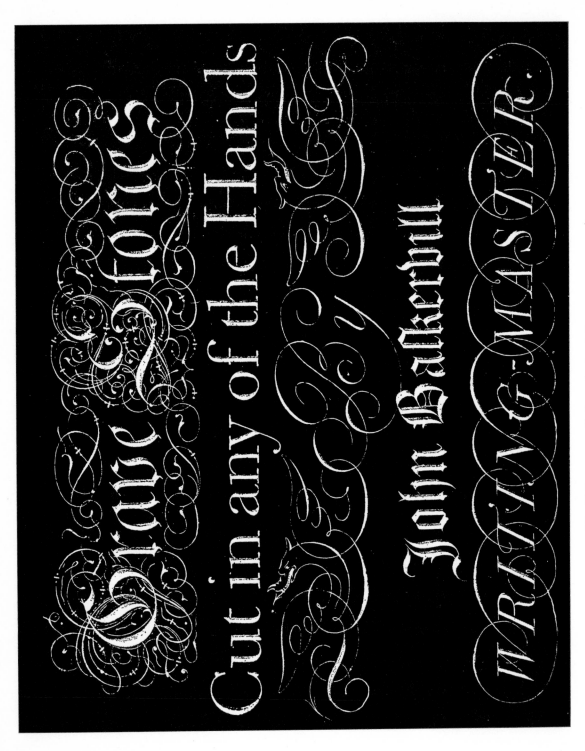

The "Gravestone" slate (*reduced from 270 × 220 mm*)

should be removed, at the expense of the parish, and preserved with the greatest care inside the church. Whether his advice was taken, no one knows; what is certain is that there is now at St. Mary's no gravestone which has any similarity to his description, either inside or outside the church.

The other was in the church of St. Bartholomew, Edgbaston (again, at that time just outside Birmingham, now a suburb). Pye says:

> There was in this church-yard a grave-stone, cut by the hands of that celebrated typographer, Baskerville, (who was originally a stone-cutter and afterwards kept a school in Birmingham), which is now removed and placed withinside the church. The stone being of a flaky nature, the inscription is not quite perfect, but whoever takes delight in looking at well-formed letters, may here be highly gratified; it was erected to the memory of Edw. Richards, an idiot, who died 21st September, 1728, with the following inscription:
>
> *If innocents are the favourites of Heaven*
> *And God but little asks where little's given,*
> *My great Creator has for me in store*
> *Eternal joys; what wise man can have more?*[1]

That is the beginning of another of the insoluble mysteries which surround Baskerville. There is no entry in the parish register for 1728 for the burial of anyone called Richards, whether Edw. or an idiot; and in 1852 there was an entry in *Notes & Queries*[2] where a correspondent signing himself RT from Warrington says that Baskerville was once foreman to a stonemason and cut some lines for the tombstone of a poor idiot who was buried at Edgbaston. He then quotes the lines, almost as Pye gives them, and goes on:

> A few days since (Jan. 26), being at Birmingham, I visited Edgbaston churchyard, and on making inquiries for the above-mentioned tombstone, was grieved to learn (from one who resembled the sexton) that nothing had been heard of it since 1816 [two years before Pye said that he saw the gravestone in the church]. It seems that, with many

---

[1] Pye: pp. 191–2. [2] N. & Q. 1st series, Vol. 5, p. 209.

other tombstones, it had been maliciously broken and destroyed in the said year, and that though a reward had been offered for the detection of the criminals, they had never been discovered . . .

In 1876 W. G. Ward contributed another version to *Notes & Queries*:[1]

. . . He carved the inscription that was to surmount his tomb with his own hand. Whether it occupied that place I cannot say; but, about forty years ago, I saw the said stone for sale in a broker's shop in Birmingham. As a boy I admired the beauty of the letters and the quaintness of the epitaph.

He then quotes a slightly different version of the epitaph above. But later in the same volume Samuel Timmins, the Birmingham antiquarian, points out that the lines did not come from Baskerville's own tomb, "but were cut by Baskervile, and, it is rumoured, were written by him . . ."[2]

Again, there is no gravestone which could be the one referred to, either inside or outside the church at Edgbaston.

It is, of course, impossible to tell whether Baskerville actually cut his gravestones: stone-cutting is not a skill that can be acquired as easily, for example, as writing—even writing as handsomely as he did. One would have thought that an apprenticeship to a stone-cutter would have been necessary (the blank period between 1706 and 1726 is amply long enough for this) but he himself later in life said, "I was brought up to no kind of business; but had early in life a great fondness for print characters." He may merely have designed and marked out the stones, employing a trained man to do the actual cutting. Whatever the real facts, he must have been in a fairly small way of business, for he does not appear in the rate-books of the town until 1733.

This makes the reason for the mortgage indenture of 1728 rather obscure. It has generally been assumed that his father and he mortgaged the Wolverley property in order to raise money for the young John to set himself up in business. Cave[3] is in no doubt about this:

[1] N. & Q. 5th series, Vol. 5, p. 373 et seq.
[2] N. & Q. 5th series, Vol. 5, p. 471.
[3] Cave: p. 27 et seq.

Soon after coming of age. . . . he must have prevailed upon his father to mortgage his estate in Upton, no doubt for him to enter into business in Birmingham. A Mortgage Indenture is recorded in the M.C.R. [Manorial Court Roll] dated 4th day of June A.D. 1728 . . . between John Baskervile the Elder, of the parish of Wolverley . . . yeoman, and John Baskervile, the Younger of Birmingham, in the Co. of Warwick, son and heir apparent of said John Baskervile, the Elder . . . on the one part, and Richard Thompson of Hampton Lovett . . . on the other part . . . in consideration of £200 . . .

It is a fairly large sum of money, and rather more than would have been needed to set up what must have been a small teaching establishment. Even when Baskerville's name does appear in the rate-books of the town, he was paying only 6d.

He must have found a reasonable number of pupils, for Birmingham at that time was a flourishing town, well into the boom which caused it to treble its population during Baskerville's lifetime. Hutton wrote in 1780:

I first came to Birmingham in 1741 . . . the buildings in the exterior of Birmingham rose in a style of elegance. Thatch, so plentiful in other towns, was not to be met with in this. I was surprised at the place, but more so at the people; They were a species I had never seen: They possessed a vivacity I had never beheld: I had been among dreamers, but now I saw men awake: Their very step along the street showed alacrity: Every man seemed to know and prosecute his own affairs: The town was large and full of inhabitants, and those inhabitants full of industry . . .[1]

The town was acting as a magnet for the whole of the surrounding area, attracting not only from the villages in the immediate neighbourhood, but from much farther afield.

Baskerville continued his career as writing-master for some years in the same area, appearing regularly in the rate-books as "John Baskervill —for School, o. o. 6d." In 1738 his father died and it is perhaps more than a coincidence that in the same year he moved to a house for which

[1] Hutton: p. 63.

he paid rates of 7d. As Cave says,[1] "in the year of his father's death, 1738, the whole of the aforegiven estates became that of his son. A most substantial and profitable holding . . . thus providing him with a fair income, for over 25 years."

It must have been about this time that Baskerville entered the japanning trade, in which he was to make a handsome living for the rest of his life. Nichols[2] and Hansard[3] both say he began his japanning career in 1745, but this is very unlikely as in 1742 he submitted a petition for a patent which clearly indicates a considerable expertise and experience in the processes of the trade:

A.D. 1742   No. 582

Machinery for Rolling and Grinding Metal Plates or Veneers.

Baskerville's Specification

To all to whom these presents shall come, John Baskerville of Birmingham, in the County of Warwick, Japanner, sendeth greeting. Whereas His present Majesty, by His Royal Letter Patent, under the Great Seal of Great Britain, bearing date the Sixteenth day of January, in the fifteenth year of his reign, hath given and granted unto me, the said John Baskerville, my exors, admors, and assigns, the sole licence and priviledge of useing, exercising, and vending a new Invention of "Making and Flatt Grinding by a Machine thin Metal Plates, and of Working or Fashioning the same, by the help of Iron Rolls and Swages, either into Mouldings (of any Size or Form) or Planes, as exactly true and level as the best Joyner could perform the like in Wood, which I propose to Japan or Varnish when so Ground and Fashioned, and to apply the same to the following subjects (to wit), to Veneir the Frames of Printings and Pictures of all Sizes, Looking Glass Frames, the Fronts of Cabinets, Buroes, Escritores, Desks, Book Cases, Toiletts, and Dressing Tables, Cupboards, Clock Cases, Weather-glass Frames, Chimney Pieces, and Wainscott and every other sort of Household Furniture now usually veneired with Ebony, Whale Bone, Walnutt, Mahogany, Pear-tree, or otherwise (the said

---

[1] Cave: p. 22 et seq.   [2] Nichols: *Lit. Anec.* III, p. 450.
[3] Hansard: p. xii.

Plates so prepared and Japanned or Varnished being more Beautiful and Durable, and in all respects answer better than anything which has hitherto been applyed to the same purpose, as the same will produce a fine glowing Mahogany Colour, a Black no way inferior to that of the most perfect India Goods, or an Imitation of Tortoiseshell which greatly excells Nature itself both in Colour and Hardness, and each Colour admitting of the most perfect Polish, whose Beauty, without violence, will not be impaired in several Ages . . .

There follows a further two and a half pages of description of the machinery. The patent was "Inrolled the Sixth day of May, in the year above written".

The japanning trade was one of Birmingham's chief industries of the period. The leading manufacturer was a Mr. Taylor who is usually credited with having introduced the trade to the town; and an almost certainly apocryphal story used to be told that Baskerville, when he decided to follow the same line of business, followed Taylor around among his suppliers, buying the same materials as he bought. With the ingredients and information thus acquired, he set up as a rival to Taylor.

Essentially, the japanning trade was the decorating of metal articles with coats of varnish. The better articles were decorated with paintings of all kinds, and Baskerville employed among others the painter Amos Green (1734–1807) who was born in Halesowen.

Some writers on Baskerville have said that he gave up his japanning activities when he started to print, suggesting that he had made a sufficient fortune to live on for the rest of his days. This is untrue, and he continued his japanning at least until 1773.

Samuel Derrick, in a letter written to the Earl of Cork, July 15, 1760, containing a description of Birmingham, says:

This ingenious artist carries on a great trade in the japan way, in which he showed me several useful articles, such as candle-sticks, stands, salvers, waiters, bread-baskets, tea-boards &c. elegantly designed, and highly finished.

Baskerville is a great cherisher of genius, which, wherever he finds it, he loses no opportunity of cultivating. One of his workmen has

9

manifested fine talents for fruit-painting, in several pieces which he shewed me.[1]

And in 1766 he was advertising in *Aris*[2] that a "Samuel Clayton, apprentice to J. Baskerville, japanner, deserted his master's service on the 1st March". The year afterwards he was again advertising that this time "On the 11th of April the following gentlemen painters, apprentices to Mr. Baskerville of Birmingham, deserted their master's service, to wit, Samuel Clayton . . . James Pinfield from Bromsgrove . . . Charles Lewis, from Gloucester . . . Samuel Jackson." He also added, the following week: "To supply the above deficiency, any boy of a decent family, who has a genius and turn for drawing, will be taken on trial on moderate terms. Any painter, of tolerable abilities, may have constant employment."

In Sketchley's Directory, 1770, appears the following entry: "Baskerville, John. Japanner of Tea Tables, Waiters, Trays etc. and Printer, Easy Hill."

In 1771 he received an order from Mrs. Mary Stovin, toy-shop keeper of 139 in Cheapside in London. It had been sent to Boulton and Fothergill "with an order for goods of our own manufacture, and accompanied with Mrs. Mary Stovin's request that we would give it to a manufacturer who would serve her well with japann'd goods . . . we have advised her that we have given her order to you & recommended you to her as one who will use her well." Baskerville replied rather tersely that he made none of the goods ordered except bread baskets.[3] Only eighteen months before his death, he wrote in a letter (now in the Assay Office, Birmingham) to Matthew Boulton:

Easy Hill 20th July 1773

Dear Sir,

I consider the prices below less than Value of the Goods, but act discretionally, but without Disct

Yrs etc John Baskerville.

[1] Derrick: p. 3.
[2] Monday, 16th June.
[3] Jay: pp. 27–8.

Nº 1 & 2	2 Trays oval fruit	6.	6.	–
Nº 3	A 32 Inch fine tray fruit (oval)	5.	5.	–
Nº 4	an oval Flower-piece 30 Inch	2.	12.	6
Nº 5	a Pastoral 34 Inch Oval	3.	3.	–
Nº 6	A fine Fruit piece	£5.	5.	–

Nº 7   Agamemnon sacrifising his Daughter
Iphegenia, who is carried away in a Cloud by
Minerva, & a Hind left upon the Altar £6. 6. –

N.B. on Sale or return

Bennett[1] suggests that at this period Baskerville had stopped manufacturing his japanned wares and was using Boulton to sell off his stock.

There is no known example extant of Baskerville's japanned goods—a rather surprising fact, if one looks at the cost of the articles listed in the letter above. They were very expensive; certainly not intended for everyday use—possibly not for use at all. And it is surprising that none has ever been identified. It has been suggested that he did his japanning on metal which had not been tinned and that the ware rusted away.[2] A more likely explanation is that none were signed, or identified in any way, and that we just do not recognise them.

An indication of Baskerville's improving fortunes is the move he made in 1740 to a house in Moor Street, where he paid a rate of 1s. 4d. and a ground rent of 18s. He appears still to have kept the tenancy of his former school in Edgbaston Street. The final indication of his increased wealth and financial security came in 1747 when, on 7th November, he signed a lease for ninety-nine years, at an annual rent of fifteen pounds and ten shillings, for

the land called or known by the name of the Binges heretofore in Three but now into four parts divided containing by Estimation seven acres or thereabouts . . . bounded on the south side by part of a common road or highway leading from New Street in Birmingham . . . to or towards Stourbridge on the east, and part of the north side by another road or highway leading from New Street . . . to or towards Dudley . . .

[1] Bennett: II, p. 39.
[2] John Lewis: *The Anatomy of Printing* (1970), p. 142.

Almost the most interesting thing about this lease is that in it Basker-ville is described as a "Boxmaker". The land was in the parish of St. Martin's and was just outside the town in the area known as "the Foreign", Birmingham at that time consisting of two Manors, the "Borough" and "the Foreign". It is now right in the centre of the city, bounded roughly by Broad Street (the road leading to Stourbridge), King Alfred's Place, and Summer Row (the road leading to Dudley). It is occupied mainly by the City's War Memorial, part of the City's administrative office (called Baskerville House) and some blocks of flats.

Baskerville agreed in the lease to spend not less than £400 on building during the years 1747–51 and he must have caused his builders to begin their work immediately he had signed the lease, for he moved into what was now called "Easy Hill" in 1748. It is possible that the name for the house came from the hill at the edge of the property: it is certainly true that this road is less steep than the road also leading away from Birming-ham about half a mile to the east. One of the roads in the very near neighbourhood was until quite recently known as Easy Row.

In his will[1] Baskerville says that he "laid out little less than £6000 on the premises" and he seems to have been proud both of the house and the grounds. In the Birmingham Assay Office there is a bill dated 6th November, 1766 for £2. 10. 0. worth of seed bought from James Gordon, a seedsman of Fenchurch Street in London.

In 1758 Baskerville received a visit from Dr. Alexander Carlyle who was on his way back to Scotland from London:

> We . . . passed the day in seeing what remained unseen at Birming-ham, particularly the Baskerville press, and Baskerville himself, who was a great curiosity. His house was a quarter of a mile from the town, and, in its way, handsome and elegant. What struck us most was his first kitchen, which was most completely furnished with everything that could be wanted, kept as clean and bright as if it had come straight from the shop, for it was used, and the fineness of the kitchen was a great point in the family; for they received their company, and there we were entertained with coffee and chocolate.[2]

[1] see pp. 122–6. [2] Carlyle: pp. 368–9.

Carlyle's companions on this visit were William Robertson, who published his *History of Scotland* the following year, and James Adam, the youngest of the four Adam brothers. John Hume, whose tragedy *Douglas* had been produced in 1756, did not visit Easy Hill (although he was one of Carlyle's companions on the trip) as he had gone to visit Admiral Smith near Hagley.

In 1760, writing to the Earl of Cork, Samuel Derrick said:

> ... his house stands at about half a mile's distance, on an eminence that commands a fine prospect. I paid him a visit, and was received with great politeness, though an entire stranger: his apartments are elegant; his stair-case is particularly curious; and the room in which he dines, and calls a Smoking room is very handsome; the grate and furniture belonging to it are, I think, of bright wrought iron and cost him a round sum ...[1]

In a letter written on 13th October, 1775, the German physicist, Lichtenberg, who was on an extended visit to this country describes how he visited Birmingham:

> ... in order to see Mr Baskerville who, as I first learnt there, already had been buried for half a year and more. I made my visit to his widow, an admirable woman ... She lives in a fine house outside the town, where she has her factory, kitchen garden and pleasure grounds, with magnificent walks between trees and laurel hedges. The rooms are furnished with the greatest taste and in all one sees wealth displayed with the wisest moderation, which shows people of taste that it has not been inherited, but acquired through diligence ...[2]

According to Noble, Baskerville "was in the habit of receiving the finest specimens of writing from the most eminent masters; which were handsomely framed and glazed, and made pleasing ornaments to one of his apartments".[3]

When Easy Hill was sold in 1788, after Mrs. Baskerville's death, the auctioneer's description of the property was:

[1] Derrick: pp. 2–3.   [2] see pp. 135–6 for full text.
[3] Noble: II, p. 361.

Easy Hill, Birmingham, consisting of a large handsome hall with an elegant mahogany staircase and gallery, three wainscotted parlours, one 19 feet by 15, the others 15 feet square, and two china closets on the floor, three exceeding good bed chambers the size of the parlours on the middle floor, and in the attic story four good lodging rooms with closets to each; marble and stone chimney pieces throughout the house and good cellars. The out Offices consist of a large Kitchen, with Servants' Rooms over it, a Butler's and common Pantry, Brewhouse, two Pumps, one hard and the other soft Water, a four-stalled Stable and Coach House, a good Garden with Green House and Garden House, spacious Warehouses and Workshops, suitable for Mercantile Business or any extensive manufactory, together with about seven Acres of rich Pasture Land in high condition, part of which is laid out in Shady Walks adorned with Shrubberies, Fish Ponds and Grotto; the whole in a Ring Fence, great part of it enclosed by a Brick Wall, and is, on account of its elevated situation and near affinity to the Canal, a very desirable spot to Build upon.

As soon as Baskerville moved into Easy Hill, Sarah Eaves went to live with him, and continued to do so till the end of his life. Her maiden name was Ruston and she had married Richard Eaves on 17th August, 1724 when she was sixteen. She had five children, one of whom had died before she went to live with Baskerville. Richard Eaves was a ne'er-do-well, deserted Sarah in 1745 and left the town. Eaves returned to Birmingham in 1762 and died in 1764 (he was buried at Yardley on 7th May). On Monday, 4th June, 1764, *Aris* carried a note:

Birmingham, June 4
On Friday last Mr. Baskerville of this Town, was married to Mrs. Eaves, Widow of the late Richard Eaves, Esq; deceased.

This living for sixteen years with a woman who was not his wife may well be one of the reasons for the barely concealed antipathy that many contemporary and nineteenth century writers show for Baskerville. In this, and in other ways, he flouted convention—and one suspects that he suffered for it during his lifetime, as his reputation certainly suffered after his death. It is also possible that some of the contemporary disapproval of his type-face may have been due as much to moral as to aesthetic reasons.

He was not, however, completely ostracised in his home town. In 1749 he was appointed Overseer of the Highways and in 1761 was made High Bailiff of the town. Yet he must have been the object of gossip and malice while occupying these public offices. On Monday, 29th January, 1750, *Aris* printed the following letter:

Birmingham, Jan 27, 1749

Whilst a malicious Report prevail'd that Mr. Baskerville was some Time ago arrested in an Action of Debt for 500l. he treated it with the Neglect and Contempt he thought due to it; but since a certain Person declared, in Moor-Street, Birmingham, to a large Company, That on Wednesday last the said Baskerville was under an Arrest for 50l. and that the Person had told him so, saw him in the Hands of the Bailiffs, (Had any body enquir'd who was the Creditor? who the Attorney? the Slander must have stopp'd here,) and that he went off on Thursday Morning; Baskerville, convinc'd by a great Variety of Informations, that the said Report is becoming general, thinks it Time to inform his Friends, that he hopes the said Rumour will do him no great Disservice; the Money he owes in the Currency of his Trade being so little, that he can pay it all at Sight: His Correspondents, on the other hand, on whom he has Demands, can every one of them testify, that he never sends them a Bill unask'd for, or till he has given a decent Credit; he is therfore greatly surpriz'd how such a Story can gain any Kind of Belief: Nevertheless, as such a villainous Scheme may ruin a Man greatly his superior in Fortune, that has large Credit, he is determin'd, in Vindication of his own Character, and to prevent, as far as he is able, so detestable a practice for the future, to prosecute, with the utmost Severity the Law will give him Leave, any one on whom the inventing or publishing the above Calumny can be fairly fix'd. Whoever can discover the Author of it, or give a Clew, by which he may be trac'd, will, by informing him, lay him under the highest Obligations of Gratitude, which will ever be acknowledged,

By his most obedient Servant,

John Baskerville

And on February 9th, 1761, there was another:

I have often wished an additional Article of the Litany, for the Use of Tradesmen: *From bad Debts and Bankrupts, Good Lord deliver us.* How deplorable is the Situation of an honest Man, who by unavoidable Misfortunes, by Errors in Judgment, or by an enterprising Turn to Business, outruns his Capital; or by other Means becomes a Bankrupt, and his Family reduced to Poverty and Distress; to say nothing of those who suffer by him. How much does he deserve our Pity; and yet how wantonly cruel are malicious and giddy Tongues in the Licence they have taken of late, with the Characters of Men in Trade.

A man can scarcely go to London, unless he publish his Intention to the whole Town, but he is gone off.

A Rascal or two of late have been taken up for Money-Making; a likeness of Name or Neighbourhood, has brought into Question Men of Reputation and Fortune.

It is but a few Years since a Carpenter, who, with a small Fortune, was utterly ruined by unluckily being of the same Name with a Man whose Affairs were bad, though in another Branch of Business, and is now a Journeyman in London.

Were this the Business of the Tea-Table only, where the Ladies, by long Prescription, claim a Right to Scandal, it should yet be confined to their own Sex; to Intrigue, Dress, Awkwardness &c. But they should not forget, that where the Breath of their Mouths may ruin the Credit, and with it the Fortune of their Neighbour, it is the worst Sort of Stinking Breath. It is surely the Duty of every Man, to suppress and discourage every Intimation to the Prejudice of his Neighbour's Credit: Would every one lend a helping Hand, this cursed Vice would soon become unfashionable, and die of itself; but as this is rather to be wished than hoped for, these flippant-tongued Gentry should be informed how heinous this Offence is deemed in the Eye of the Law. Presumptive Damages have been given without Proof:

The late Mr. Brooks recovered 400l. of Mr. Mason, late of Stratford, for traducing his Character. If the least Injury is proved, a Jury will give ample Damages, Cost of Suit follows; but if no Damage is proved, the Plaintiff is Sure of a Verdict: Every one that tells the Tale, is a Publisher, and liable to Prosecution, no Matter who was the Inventor. As your Paper is calculated for the Public, I doubt not but you will give the above a Place in it.

Yours

J.B.

There are not many contemporary references to Baskerville's character available, and of these most are scanty, confining themselves, as Derrick did, to a reference to Baskerville's hospitality.[1] Kippis says much the same:

> The writer of this article can add his own testimony concerning Mr. Baskerville's politeness to strangers, and the cheerful hospitality with which he treated those who were introduced to him . . .[2]

Carlyle, who visited him in 1758, suggests that Baskerville had some snobbishness in his make-up and makes it quite clear that people varied in their assessment of him:

> Hume's absence afflicted him, for he had seen and heard of the tragedy of *Douglas*. Robertson hitherto had no name, and the printer said bluntly that he would rather have one subscription to his work of a man like Mr. Hume, than a hundred ordinary men. He dined with us that day, and acquitted himself so well that Robertson pronounced him a man of genius, while James Adam and I thought him but a prating pedant.[3]

Mark Noble has no good word to say about him:

> I have very often been with my father at his house, and found him ever a most profane wretch, and ignorant of literature to a wonderful degree. I have seen many of his letters, which, like his will, were not written grammatically; nor could he even spell well. In person he was a shrivelled old coxcomb. His favourite dress was green, edged with narrow gold lace; a scarlet waistcoat, with very broad gold lace; and a small round hat, likewise edged with gold lace. His wife was all

[1] see p. 13.   [2] Kippis: I, p. 672.
[3] Carlyle: p. 368.

17

that affectation can describe. She lived in adultery with him many years. She was originally a servant. Such a pair are rarely met with. He had wit; but it was always at the expence of religion and decency, particularly if in company with the clergy. I have often thought there was much similarity in his person to Voltaire, whose sentiments he was ever retailing . . .[1]

The only example of Baskerville's wit which seems to have survived is that quoted in a letter about The Leasowes (William Shenstone's house at Halesowen) in *The Gentleman's Magazine* for August, 1823, p. 105:

. . . Several of the rooms were fitted up in Gothic style, in which he evinced great taste; and one was painted to imitate trellis-work, overhung with hazel-trees, &c. This room produced the following anecdote.

Mr. Baskerville, who was intimate with Shenstone, one day took his friend Dr. S——ll to see the Leasowes. After admiring the tasteful disposition of the grounds, Mr. Shenstone conducted them into the house to take some refreshment, which was prepared in the room alluded to. "How admirably this apartment is fitted up," exclaimed Dr. S——ll. "Those surely cannot be artificial (pointing to one of the walls:)—they must be real hazel-nuts."—"Wall-nuts, if you please," replied Mr. B. drily. For once the *sombre* countenance of Shenstone disappeared, and, after various efforts to suppress a smile, he at length left the room in a complete laugh.[2]

The fairest, and probably the most accurate, account of his character is that written by William Hutton, who had lived in Birmingham for the last twenty-five years of Baskerville's life. He wrote the first history of the town (which Hill[3] rather uncharitably describes as being regarded "as an authority by those who prefer fiction to accuracy and pleasant fallacies to truth") but in the first part of his article printed in *The European Magazine* for November, 1785, he gives an almost completely accurate account of Baskerville's life and goes on:

[1] Noble: pp. 361–2.
[2] I am indebted to Mr. J. Hunt for drawing this letter to my attention.
[3] Hill: p. 55.

In private life he was a humourist, idle in the extreme, but his invention was of the true Birmingham model, active. He could well design, but procured others to execute; wherever he found merit he caressed it: he was remarkably polite to the stranger, fond of shew: a figure rather of the smaller size, and delighted to adorn that figure with gold lace.—Although constructed with the light timbers of a frigate, his movement was solemn as a ship of the line.

During the twenty-five years I knew him, though in the decline of life, he retained the singular traces of a handsome man. If he exhibited a peevish temper we may consider good-nature and intense thinking are not always found together.

Taste accompanied him through the different walks of agriculture, architecture and the fine arts. Whatever passed through his fingers, bore the lively marks of John Baskerville.

His aversion to Christianity would not suffer him to lie among Christians; he therefore erected a mausoleum in his own grounds for his remains; and died without issue in 1775, at the age of 69 . . .

Invention seldom pays the inventor. If you ask what fortune Baskerville ought to have been rewarded with? The most which can be comprised in five figures. If you further ask what he possessed? The least; but none of it squeezed from the press. What will the shade of the great man think, if capable of thinking, that he has spent a fortune of opulence, and a life of genius, in carrying to perfection the greatest of all human inventions, and that his productions, slighted by his country, were hawked over Europe in quest of a bidder . . .

This seems to be the primary source for all subsequent writers about Baskerville's character. Some of them have the grace to give Hutton credit; some quote him word for word with no acknowledgement of any sort.

In the Birmingham Reference Library, on the letter written by Baskerville to Livie in 1766[1] there is a note by Catherine Hutton, daughter of William Hutton:

Fine printing was first introduced by John Baskerville, who lived,

[1] see p. 101.

and printed, and died, at Birmingham, and was buried in his own ground, in what he had erected as a paper mill. I remember him, and his gold laced waistcoat, and his pair of cream-coloured horses, and his painted chariot, each pannel a picture, fresh from his own manufactory of japanned tea-boards. I also remember him by the token that he once took me up in his arms and kissed me. Baskerville's paper was excellent, as well as his types. Printing paper is now [1836] made of cotton rags and plaster of Paris, and bleached with various acids.

Hill was, of course, writing at the end of the nineteenth century and says little of Baskerville's character, but he does mention of Baskerville and Boulton in 1766:

Both attended the funeral at that church [St. Philip's, now the Cathedral Church of Birmingham] of John Wyatt, of cotton-spinning fame, Baskerville wearing on the occasion a gold-laced coat as a protest, it is said, against superstitious custom.[1]

Baskerville is wearing a gold-laced coat in the portrait by James Millar painted in 1774. The colours of his clothes have darkened in the two hundred years of the painting's existence, but the clothes he is wearing are obviously very similar to those mentioned by Noble.

The Millar portrait is the origin of all the other portraits we still know. Hansard[2] described how he arranged for Samuel Raven to copy the Millar painting, and this was again copied and engraved on wood for use in *Typographia*. The Raven portrait is that in the National Portrait Gallery, and although Bennett said[3] in 1939 that the owner of the Millar portrait was unknown at that time, it was presented to the City of Birmingham Art Gallery in 1940 by the Rev. A. H. Caldicott.

Hansard[2] said that relations and friends of Baskerville's step-daughter who were still living at the time he was arranging for the Raven copy to be made "consider this likeness [i.e. the Millar portrait] of Mr. Baskerville to be a most excellent and faithful resemblance".

One hopes it is: for the face shows determination and some obstinacy,

[1] Hill: p. 61.   [2] Hansard: p. xiii.
[3] Bennett: II, p. 118.

but there is a sparkle in the eye that argues a sense of humour. The lips are compressed and the mouth turns down at the corners, but it looks as if it might as easily turn up. Being perhaps over-fanciful, one might imagine that Sarah had persuaded him into having the portrait done: he is sitting there, looking as serious as he can, wondering how much the portrait will cost him, pretending disapproval but secretly flattered by the whole affair.

It is strange, in view of his notorious anti-established religion views, that Baskerville apparently played a part in the management of St. Philip's church. He signed minutes in the Vestry Book on at least two occasions—1750 and 1751—recommending the expenditure of money on the purchase of bells for the church. It may be that his anti-church views did not crystallise till later in his life, or that his official position in the town required him to take part. It may even be that Sarah, whom one assumes to have been a regular church-goer as she is buried in St. Philip's churchyard, may have been the reason; though one doubts if her status at this time would have made her particularly welcome in a church which was always the most fashionable of the town's churches.

There is an interesting item of information from this period mentioned in a book by J. A. Langford called *A Century of Birmingham Life* . . . (Birmingham, 1868). He was writing in the 1860s, or, more correctly, assembling quotations from *Aris's Birmingham Gazette* and came across a poem printed in the paper on 28th January 1751:

It is written in the manner of Spenser, and as a literary production is not without considerable merit. Its chief attraction to us, however, is that we have in this poem the effect which the town then produced on a thoughtful and cultivated mind . . .

INDUSTRY AND GENIUS;
OR, THE
ORIGIN OF BIRMINGHAM.
A Fable
Attempted in the Manner of Spencer.
Inscribed to Mr. B——

I.

O B——! in whom, tho' rare, unite
The Spirit of Industrie and eke the Ray
Of bright inventive Genius; while I write,
Do Thou with Candour listen to the Lay
Which to fair Birmingham the Muse shall pay,
Marking, beneath a Fable's thin Disguise,
The Virtues its Inhabitants display;
Those Virtues, whence their Fame, their Riches rise,
Their nice mechanic Arts, their various Merchandise . . .
[There are seven stanzas in all]

Langford continues, "We should very much like to know who was the author of this poem. The Mr. B. to whom it was inscribed was the famous Birmingham printer, John Baskerville."[1] The poem was also printed in *The London Magazine* in January 1751 (pp. 37–8) with Baskerville's name written out in full.

Whether the praise in the first three lines was justified at the time the poem was written, it was soon to be more than justified.

[1] Vol. I, pp. 38–40.

2

It must have been about this time, or even earlier (see his letter written in 1757[1] and the draft letter of 1775[2]) that Baskerville began his experiments in printing. The letter he wrote to Robert Dodsley (among the best-known of contemporary London booksellers) in October 1752 indicates that he had already made considerable progress in both type and press:

Birmingham 2^d Oct. 1752

Dear S^r

To remove in some measure y^r Impatience I have sent you an impression of 14 Punches of the two-line Great Primer, which have been begun and finish'd in 9 Days only, & contain all the Letters Roman necessary in the Titles and half Titles. I can't forbear saying they please me, as I can make nothing more correct, nor shall you see anything of mine much less so. You'll observe they strike the Eye much more sensibly than the smaller Characters tho Equally perfect, till the press shows them to more Advantage. The press is creeping slowly towards perfection; I flatter myself with being able to print nearly as good a colour & smooth a stroke as the inclos'd; I should esteem it a favour if you'd send me the Initial Letters of all the Cantos lest they should not be included in the said 14, & three or four pages of any Part of the Poem from whence to form a Bill for the casting a suitable number of each letter: The R wants a few slight Touches and the Y half an hour's Correction. This day we have

---

[1] see p. 43.   [2] see p. 140.

resolutely set about 15 of the same siz'd Italick Capitals, which will not be at all inferior to the Roman, & I doubt not to compleat them in a fortnight. You need therefore be in no pain about our being ready by the time appointed. Our best Respects to Mrs Dodsley & our friend M^r. Becket, concludes me

Y^r most obed^t serv^t
John Baskerville
Verte

Pray put it in no one's power to let M^r. Caslon see them.

The remark at the beginning of the letter about impressions of punches refers to the punch-cutter's method of testing his punches by holding the punch above a candle-flame for a second or two to coat it with carbon and pressing it on a piece of paper. In fact, in his next letter to Dodsley, Baskerville actually refers to "Impressions from a Candle".

These punches are the heart of any typefounding process done by hand. Essentially, what the punch-cutter does is to take a piece of steel two or three inches long and roughly square in section. At one end of this he cuts, using engraving tools, files, counter-punches, a representation of the letter. When this is completed to his satisfaction, the punch is hardened and driven into a block of copper, forming a matrix from which the actual printing-type is cast. Delicate, scrupulous craftsmanship, coupled with a high degree of aesthetic sensibility, are only the beginnings of the punch-cutter's qualities. F. C. Avis, writing about *Edward Prince*, (London 1967), the great punch-cutter who cut much of the type for the Kelmscott, Doves and Ashendene presses, says that an expert punch-cutter was supposed to average about a punch and a half a day, but that one a day would be more realistic.

It is doubtful if Baskerville cut his own punches even though he must have supervised their cutting with great care. In a letter written in 1757 he says:

I have pursued the Scheme of printing and Letter founding for Seven Years, with the most intense Application, to the great prejudice of My Eyes, by the daily use of Microscopes . . .[1]

[1] See pp. 43–4 for full text.

Some of the original roman punches, now at the Cambridge University Press. The punches are shown lying on a replica of the 1777 type specimen

It is fairly certain that his punch-cutter was John Handy. The *Gentleman's Magazine* carried a note of his death: "Towards the end of 1792 died Mr. John Handy, the artist who cut the punches for Baskerville's types . . ." He must have joined Baskerville very early in the printing project, for there is a reference to him in the draft of a letter written for Sarah Baskerville after the printer's death:

> Mrs Baskerville hath ye very honest man which performed all ye manual opperations both in respect of fileing ye punchions, making ye letter moulds & every other improvement which Mr Baskerville made in printing. He hath worked with Mr Baskervill upwards of 28 years. . . .[1]

This letter was written in 1775 and even if the clerk in Matthew Boulton's office who wrote the letter was exaggerating, it still shows that John Handy (and one must assume that it is he who is "ye very honest man") joined Baskerville well before 1750.

The other interesting reference in Baskerville's letter to Dodsley is "the smaller characters". It looks very much as if Baskerville had already cut some smaller letters than the two-line Great Primer, which was one of the three types which were used in the first specimen (issued in 1754) of the Quarto Virgil. One wonders, too, if the reference to Caslon is serious or playful.

Just over a fortnight later, Baskerville again wrote to Dodsley:

> Birmingham, 19 Oct, 1752
>
> Dear S^r,
>
> As I propos'd in my last I have sent you Impressions from a Candle of 20 two lines Great Primer Italick, which were begun & finish'd in 10 Days only, we are now about figures which are in a good forwardness, & changing a few of those Letters we concluded finish'd. My next care will be to strike the Punches into Copper & justify them with all the care and skill I am master of. You may depend on my being ready by ye time (Christmas) but if more time could be allow'd I should make use of it all in correcting & justifying: as so much

---

[1] See pp. 139–41 for full text.

depends on appearing perfect on First starting; I have with great pains justified the plate for the platten & stone on which it falls, so that they are as perfect planes as it will ever be in my power to procure, for instance if you rest one end of ye plate on the stone, & let the other fall the height of an inch; it falls soft as if you dropt it on feathers or several folds of silk, and when you raise it, you manifestly feel it suck (if you'll excuse so unphilosophical a term). Wet the two and either would support the other with (I believe) 500 Wt added to it, if held perpendicularly. To so perfect a plane will I endeavour to bring the faces of the Types, if I have time, nor do I despair of better Ink & Printing than has hitherto been seen.

I must beg leave to remark on the plate sent me, that I fear the performer is capable of doing nothing much better, as he's greatly deficient in Design, Drawing & Execution with the Needle; the Composition of the Ornament, if it will bear that Name, is mean, or if you will, means nothing; To speak in my own way, the D is as bad as one can well be made. If you are determin'd to have the Initials grav'd, I would refer you to Pine's Horace, where the Execution is neat, tho' the proportion is bad; the Letter is suppos'd raised, consequently the side next the light is express'd by a very faint line, its opposite is very strong, like the light and shadow in a picture. If you'll accept my Judgm^t and skill it is at y^r service. Give me the Initials and size, or if you please I'll give the size 4, 5 or 6 Lines Great Primer, and the Letters as correct as I can draw them in black Lead, the Ornament as you and the Graver can agree. Thus Dear S^r you see I readily accept the Terms you are so kind to offer me of treating you freely as my Friend; pray consider the above as *inter nos* only, & give me a line as soon as you have leisure. As you are in the Land of Franks; half a doz. would do me a particular pleasure, as a good many things not worth a Groat might be communicated by

Y^r most obed^t hbe serv^t
J. Baskerville

Haste had almost made me forget Complim^ts of the Family, &c.

The information about the press shows Baskerville's attitude towards his project. There had been little real improvement to the printing press since Gutenberg's day: it was still essentially two flat surfaces—the "platten & stone on which it falls"—forced together by a screw. Baskerville did not change this, but he obviously was dissatisfied with what one suspects the typical eighteenth-century press to have been: a rather inaccurate, unreliable piece of apparatus on which it would be nearly impossible to produce high quality work.

The indication, in this and in the previous letter to Dodsley, is that Baskerville at this time had only one press, which he had built himself, improving certain parts of it. By the time of his death, he had four presses at least: Sarah was certainly trying to sell four printing presses late in 1775.[1]

In a letter he wrote in December, 1773, Baskerville gives some more information, with perhaps a certain lack of modesty, about his presses:[2]

> . . . my Presses &c. are exactly on the same Construction of other Peoples but perhaps more accurate than any ever formed since the Invention of the Art of Printing; to explain myself, I have been able to produce three more perfect Plans, than have before appeared in a Letter-Press; (to wit) the Stone, the Platten (mine are all of Brass an Inch thick). The two first may be produced by any Man who has some Ingenuity and much Attention; But for the third, all Printers must depend on the Letter-founder. All my presses were made at Home under my own Inspection; for the Truth of the whole Work I refer you to the enclos'd Specimen, produced at one pull of the Bar, the larger Characters fully inked, the smaller not over-inked: I use but one double of the finest Flannel, others two or three double of thick Swanskin. . . .

The reference in the last two lines is to the packing of the tympan of the press. This is a double frame which folds down over the platen and, with the frisket (another frame), holds the paper between the platen and the inked surface of the type.

John Dreyfus wrote in 1951[3] about a document he had discovered in

---

[1] see p. 141.   [2] see p. 129 for full text.
[3] Dreyfus: *Signature*, p. 45.

the Bibliothèque Nationale compiled by Etienne Anisson-Duperron. In it there is some additional information about Baskerville's presses and methods of work:

> Baskerville's tympans were fitted out entirely differently from ordinary presses. He barred all soft packing, such as the flannel which . . . "French workmen think they cannot have too much of in order to obtain what they most value, namely heavy impression; and behind which they believe they can conceal the shortcomings of their faulty workmanship." Instead, Baskerville covered his tympan with a smooth vellum and packed it with two or three layers of good superfine cloth, between which was inserted a smooth and very thin piece of cardboard . . . This matter of tympan packing was of the greatest importance. Too great a thickness would have destroyed the advantages of the precision-made brass platen and stone . . .

Improvements to the printing press and its use were not the only things on which Baskerville was spending time and ingenuity. His reference in the letter to "better Ink" is more than a pious hope. The blackness of the ink he used was one of the causes for contemporary admiration (from those of his contemporaries who did admire him).

The early nineteenth-century pundits certainly admired it. Dibdin refers to Baskerville's ink as "partaking of a peculiarly soft lustre, bordering upon purple"[1] and Hansard[2] says:

> It was reserved for him to discover . . . a superior kind of black for the purpose required, and to this success may be attributed, in a great measure, the superiority of his printing . . . the discovery of Baskerville, of about the year 1760, lay dormant from the time of his death till 1790, when, through Mr. Robert Martin of Birmingham, his apprentice and afterwards his foreman, a considerable quantity of this fine black which had been collecting, for a length of time, from the glass-pinchers' and solderers' lamps, was bought by him, at an almost unlimited price . . ."

[1] Dibdin: *Classics* II, p. 556 note.
[2] Hansard: pp. 717–8.

Hansard, a few pages farther on,[1] gives the method used for making the ink,

> which has never before been published . . . He took of the finest and oldest linseed oil [at this point Hansard has a foot-note of about two hundred and fifty words on linseed oil] three gallons, this was put into a vessel capable of holding four times the quantity, and boiled with a long-continued fire till it acquired a certain thickness of tenacity, according to the quality of the work it was intended to print, and which was judged of by putting small quantities upon a stone to cool, and then taking it up between the finger and thumb; on opening which, if it drew into a thread an inch long or more, it was considered sufficiently boiled . . . The oil thus prepared was suffered to cool, and had then a small quantity of black or amber rosin dissolved in it, after which it was allowed some months to subside; it was then mixed with the fine black, before named, to a proper thickness, and ground for use.

C. H. Bloy, in his *History of Printing Ink* . . . (London, 1967) suggests that the addition of resin would add sheen to the ink, and there is a statement in Anisson-Duperron's report[2] that "one of Baskerville's principles had been to keep his ink for three years before using it". Lichtenberg says, talking of Sarah Baskerville:

> Another secret of which she is just as proud as the glazing, is the recipe for her husband's black printing, which is unknown to all English printers. This differs not so much through the beauty of the colour as through this, that it dries unusually swiftly and endures glazing better and earlier than the general.[3]

But the most interesting, or perhaps—to be honest—most infuriating, reference in these letters from Baskerville to Dodsley is to the "Poem", "all the Cantos" and the comments on the "plate sent me". Patently, Baskerville is not referring to the *Virgil* of 1757. Even he, with his cult of perfection and disregard of a realistic time-scale, could not have said

[1] Hansard: pp. 722–3. [2] Dreyfus: *Signature*, p. 47.
[3] see p. 135.

that he would be ready by Christmas when in fact it was to be another five years before his book appeared.

In addition, he would be unlikely to refer to Virgil's works as the "Poem"; it is difficult to see what he meant by "Cantos"; and finally the "plate" must be an etching or engraving that was to appear in the book. There was nothing of this kind in the *Virgil*. It even looks as if the book was a joint venture between Baskerville and Dodsley, which the *Virgil* was not, although Dodsley did take 20 copies.

Engendered by frustration at one's inability to solve this mystery, all sorts of wild speculations enter the mind: is there a hitherto undiscovered work printed by Baskerville, published three or four years before the *Virgil*, still waiting to be discovered? Or did he cut several fonts of type, use these for the work, become dissatisfied with it (possibly because it was too like the type Caslon had cut) and begin all over again? It was certainly not beyond him and his stubborn search for perfection. Did he scrap all the work he had done by the end of 1752 and begin again—there is a gap of fifteen months between the letters quoted above and the next letter to Dodsley still extant. And in that letter he was still talking about the Great Primer.

Such speculation is idle, and it is much safer to assume—as everyone always has—that Baskerville, heedless of time and economic necessity, carried on with his refining of the construction of his press and its working, improving the design of his letter, experimenting with new formulae for ink, and testing methods of improving the appearance of printing papers for the next four years.

It must also be remembered, and we often tend to forget this, that Baskerville was not merely a printer and publisher. He was a manufacturer of japanned goods for nearly the whole of his working life, and although by this time he was employing Handy, presumably full-time on the printing project, this must have come second in his order of priorities. He could not have made the, comparatively, handsome fortune he left his wife at his death if he had not worked hard at his real trade. He had plenty of rivals in Birmingham in the japanning trade and must have had to concentrate much of his time and commercial acumen on keeping ahead of them. In addition to this, he seems to have had a fairly full social life and he certainly had civic responsibilities which were a call on his time.

The next letter which we still have that Baskerville wrote to Dodsley is dated 16th January, 1754:

> . . . I have put the last hand to my Great Primer, and have corrected fourteen letters in the specimen you were so kind to approve, and have made good progress in the English, and have formed a new alphabet of Two-line Double Pica and Two line Small Pica capitals for Titles, not one of which I can mend with a wish, as they come up to most perfect idea I have letters . . . [He then details his scheme for obtaining absolutely correct texts of the works he is about to print] 'Tis this, Two people must be concerned; the one must name every letter, capital, point, reference, accent, etc., that is, in English, must spell every part of every word distinctly, and note down every difference in a book prepared on purpose. Pray oblige me in making the experiment with Mr James Dodsley in four or five lines of any two editions of an author, and you'll be convinced that it's scarcely possible for the least difference, even of a point, to escape notice. I would recommend and practise the same method in an English author, where most people imagine themselves capable of correcting. Here's another advantage to me in this humble scheme; at the same time that a proof sheet is correcting, I shall find out the least imperfection in the types that has escaped the founder's notice. I have great enconiums on my Specimen from Scotland . . .[1]

In spite of Baskerville's views on proof reading, it seems unlikely that his suggestions were carried out. As Gaskell says, "most of his books were beautiful, expensive and incorrect".[2]

It was later this year that Baskerville first appears in Shenstone's letters, though from the letter itself their acquaintance must have been of some standing and intimacy. William Shenstone lived at Halesowen, at that time five miles to the west of Birmingham, now just over the city border. He was a poet of some merit and spent most of his time writing,

[1] S. & D.: pp. 95–6 (quoting T.B.R.).
[2] Gaskell: p. xix.

particularly letters to his many friends, and re-designing his garden at The Leasowes. On 29th September, 1754, he wrote to Lady Luxborough:

... When I left your Chaise at ye End of Birmingham, I propops'd only to beg a Draught of Perry at Mr. Baskerville's Door; but was soon prevail'd on to alight, and spend an hour or two very agreeably. They both seem'd extremely sorry that your Ladyship had not *time* to call; which I assur'd them was the Case. I found them sitting in their Parlour with a Busto-maker hard at work in finishing the Bustos of Mr. and Mrs Baskerville; 'serving God with his Talent,' as I think was Sir Godfrey Kneller's Phrase, when he painted on Sunday. The Bustos are greatly like . . .[1]

During 1754 Baskerville issued specimens or prospectuses for the *Virgil*. Gaskell records five variations,[2] some showing the proposed title-page and a page of text, one (see p. 34) showing a setting from Melmoth's translation of Cicero's *Letters to his Friends*.[3] He was to use some of the same text in his first type specimen of 1757.

In December of this year there was an advertisement in *The Norwich Mercury* which, except for few minor changes in wording (and the names of "Mr Richard Taylor and W. Close in Norwich, and the men who deliver this paper") is the same as the bottom paragraph on the specimen on p. 34.

Anyone who subscribed as a result of this advertisement would have had to wait for nearly two and a half years for the publication of the book, and even though printing a book of over 400 pages on a hand-press is an enormous task, one is still left with a feeling of something like awe.

In March, 1755, Shenstone writing to Dodsley hopes "Mr. Baskerville meets in London with the encouragement he deserves"[4] and in his reply Dodsley says, "Mr Baskerville's Specimen is much approved, and he has met with great encouragement at both the Universities."[5] During this time Baskerville was playing a fairly full part in civic affairs. Bennett

[1] Williams CLXX.
[2] Gaskell: pp. 3–5.
[3] Gaskell: p. ii.
[4] Williams CLXXXIII.
[5] S. & D.: p. 45.

SPECIMEN

By *JOHN BASKERVILLE* of BIRMINGHAM,

In the County of Warwick, *Letter-Founder and Printer.*

To CNEIUS PLANCIUS.

I Am indebted to you for two letters, dated from Corcyra. You congratulate me in one of them on the account you have received, that I still preserve my former authority in the commonwealth: and wish me joy in the other of my late marriage. With respect to the first, if to mean well to the interest of my country and to approve that meaning to every friend of its liberties, may be considered as maintaining my authority; the account you have heard is certainly true. But if it consists in rendering those sentiments effectual to the public welfare, or at least in daring freely to support

To *CAIUS CASSIUS,* proquæstor.

MY own inclinations have anticipated your recommendation: and I have long since received Marcus Fabius into the number of my friends. He has extremely endeared himself to me indeed, by his great politeness and elegance of manners: but particularly by the singular affection I have observed he bears towards you. Accordingly, tho' your letter in his behalf was not without effect, yet my own knowledge of the regard he entertains for you had somewhat more: you may be assured therefore I shall very faithfully confer upon him the good offices you request.

TO THE PUBLIC

JOHN BASKERVILLE proposes, by the advice and assistance of several learned men, to print, from the Cambridge edition corrected with all possible care, an elegant edition of Virgil. The work will be printed in quarto, on a very fine writing royal paper, and with the above letter. The price of the Volume in sheets will be one guinea, no part of which will be required till the book is delivered. It will be put to press as soon as the number of Subscribers shall amount to five hundred, whose names will be prefixt to the work. All persons who are inclined to encourage the undertaking, are desired to send their names to JOHN BASKERVILLE in Birmingham; who will give specimens of the work to all who are desirous of seeing them.

Subscriptions are also taken in, and specimens delivered by Messieurs R. and J. DODSLEY, Booksellers in Pall Mall, London.

Type-specimen, 1754 (*reduced from 213 × 292 mm*)

records that he was "one of fifteen leading inhabitants who nominated the four overseers. The next year he was appointed 'Surveyor of the Highways' and in that year on 29th June, 1756, he was reproved for paying out £18. 10s. without authority."[1]

Just before Christmas 1756 Baskerville wrote to Dodsley:

Bir^m. 20 Decr. 1756

Dear S^r.

I have for some past hoped a line from you in Relation to the paper Scheme; whether you have sent, or chose to send any of the thin post to Mr Culver as that is the only Article I lay any Stress upon in his hands; pray do not send it, if you are more inclined to keep it; He shall stay till I can furnish him, which probably may be six Weeks or two months; I have not more than six Ream of that sort, which If I chose to do it, I could sell tomorrow in Birm^m at 24/. & if inserting his name makes the least difference in y^r Scheme of Advertising, I shall like it quite as well left out. I have sent Samples of the ornamented paper & thin post gilt to several neighbouring towns & have receiv'd Orders freely from them; I told you in my last the prices, but that need not be a Rule to you, perhaps some of y^r Customers would like them less if sold too low—all I fear'd was laying an Embargo on them. I propose Reducing the price of the octavo from 21 to 18 as it will be more suitable to the Quarto; Pray therefore make me D^r for that difference in all y^r Stock of that Sort. Pray give me y^r Opinion if it would be wrong to make a present of a quire of each sort, & the thin gilt to the Princes of Wales, As a Sample of English Manufactory to be had at Mr Dodsley's; the present mine.

I copied with great pleasure, from our Birm Paper a fine Complement. made you, which I shall learn by heart, & of which I give you Joy. I shall have Virgil out of the press by the latter End of Jan^y & hope to produce the Volume as smooth as the best Paper I have sent you. Pray will it not be proper to advertize how near it is finishing, & beg the Gentlemen who intend favouring me with their Names to send them by that time.

[1] Bennett: I, pp. 68–9.

35

When this is done; I can print nothing at home but another Classick, (a Specimen of which will be given with it) which I cannot forbear thinking a grievous hardship after the infinite pains & great expense I have been at. I have almost a mind to print a pocket Classick in one size larger than the old Elzivers as the difference will on Comparison be obvious to every Scholer nor should I be very sollicitous whether it paid me or not.

You have not fulfill'd y^r promise in sending me the printer's Scheme. I am with due Respect to Mr James Dodsley & Comp^ts of the ensuing Season

D^r S^r

Y^r obed^t Servt

J. Baskerville

The "fine Complemt" had in fact appeared in *Aris* on the same day that Baskerville wrote. It is a rather elegantly written, if somewhat mannered, poem of six stanzas:

On Tully's Head, in Pall-Mall, 1756
By the Rev. Mr. G***s.
Where Tully's Bust, and Honour'd Name
Point out the venal *Page*
There Dodsley consecrates to Fame
The Classicks of his Age.

In vain the Poets, from their Mine,
Extract the shining Mass;
Till Dodsley's Mint has stamped the Coin,
And bade the Sterling Pass . . .

Baskerville had a reply from Dodsley dated 10th February, 1757:

To Mr Baskerville.

Dear Sir

I am very sorry we seem a little to have misunderstood each other. I think I have somewhere your direction to charge Mr Culver 24^s. per Ream for whatever plain Paper he had of me; and thought, as I

36

had paid you for it, he was to pay me. However, if I am mistaken, let it be as you say, it is a matter of but small consequence, & I hope it will sell both with Mr Culver and me, he having had a second parcel. I have sent a small sortment of every kind to Mr Loake at Bath. But I beg you will take notice that if you don't stop your hand in the ornamented Paper, you will certainly be at a very great loss, as you are to take all back of that kind you know which I don't dispose of; and to tell you the truth I have not open'd a single Ream of either parcel you sent me this Winter Quarto or Octavo, & have used but very few dozens of the Messages. So that I think you should not ornament another sheet, till you see how you can dispose of what I have, & let me send it you back immediately for that purpose. As to lowering the price, I am very sorry you thought of it so late. You may remember how earnestly I press'd you to set it at first as low as possibly you could, for your own sake, and that nobody might interfere with you. But to sell it now at a lower price than we set out with, I think is hardly fair, I am sure not creditable either for you or me, and what I believe upon reflection you will hardly think proper for either of us to do. Besides, I am far from thinking it would now revive the sale. The account you give me of the Virgil pleases me much, & I hope you will in that have all the success your heart can wish. I beg if you have any objection addition or alteration to make in the following Advertisement, you will let me know by ye return of the post. If I don't hear from you I will immediately advertise. Pray let me know at ye same time about sending back the ornamented Paper.

To the Public.
John Baskerville of Birmingham thinks proper to give notice that having now finish'd his Edition of Virgil in one volume Quarto Price one Guinea in Sheets, it will be publish'd the latter end of next month. He therefore desires that such Gentlemen as intend to favour him with their Names, will be pleas'd to send them either to himself at Birmingham, or to R & J Dodsley in Pall Mall, in order that they may be inserted in the List of his Encouragers.

Even at this stage, Baskerville was still over-optimistic about the Virgil (it did not appear till April) and before it did appear a note of acrimony was to creep into the correspondence.

These letters, however, are obviously more concerned with Baskerville's paper than his books—and not the paper on which he was printing the book, although it must have been his experiments with paper for the books which led to his becoming a supplier of writing paper to Dodsley and others.

In the often quoted letter from Derrick, there is the statement, "He manufactures his own paper," which is almost certainly not true, even though Baskerville himself refers to paper "of his own manufacture". On the other hand, he must have made some experiments in the actual manufacture of paper, *The Advancement of Arts, Manufactures, and Commerce* . . . by William Bailey (London, 1772) says, on page 217:

> The Society [i.e. the Royal Society of Arts] having been informed that there is a very valuable Paper made of Silk rags, they came to a resolution to offer Two considerable Premiums for the encouragement of this Manufacture . . . The Candidates for this Manufacture were . . . Mr. Baskerville, of Birmingham.

But it is very unlikely that he could have made more than a few sheets at Easy Hill. One of the essentials in paper-making is a copious supply of water, and though there were two pumps and a fishpond at Easy Hill, a rather greater supply of water was normally needed for paper-making on a serious commercial scale.

In addition to this, he often refers to the cost of paper in terms which clearly suggest that he was buying it from a supplier. For example, in 1759, when he wrote to the Vice-Chancellor of the University of Cambridge about arrangements for printing his prayerbook there, he says, "The paper is very good & stands me in 27 or 28 shillings the Ream."[1]

A reference to Baskerville's paper in Mores gives an indication of the contemporary attitude to it, although doing nothing to solve the mystery of whether Baskerville made his own paper. Mores says: ". . . his typographical excellence lay more in trim glossy paper to dim the sight."[2] In the Appendix, John Nichols writes:

[1] see p. 64. [2] Mores: p. 81.

... His glossy paper and *too-sharp* type offend the patience of a reader more sensibly than the innovations I have already censured.

And there is a note, contributed by "a friend" about the "glossy paper":

When Baskerville came to Cambridge, we told him that the exceeding sharpness of his letter, and the glossy whiteness of his paper, both beyond any thing that we had been used to, would certainly offend; and we spoke much in praise of, and shewed him, the paper with a yellow cast, on which H. Stephen's capital editions are printed. This, he told us, he could easily imitate, and accordingly executed some sheets; but they were by no means the thing, the colouring not being uniformly dispersed, but clouded or waved like a quire of paper stained with rain ...[1]

There are two questions to be considered about Baskerville's paper: the use of "wove" paper, and his "hot-pressing". The first is a matter of manufacture; the second of treatment after it is made, or printed on.

Paper essentially is made by breaking up fibrous vegetable matter (flax, cotton, wood) into its constituent fibres, making a suspension of these fibres in water, spreading the fibre/water mixture on a fine wire mesh so that the water drains away, leaving a thin sheet of matted fibres on the mesh. This sheet, when dried and pressed, is the sheet of paper. Until the early nineteenth century all paper was made by hand, and until about the time Baskerville printed his first book, all paper was "laid". These "laid" or "wove" papers are made by using different styles of assembling the wires in the mesh of the paper-maker's mould. To produce "laid" paper, the wires are parallel and supported at intervals by thicker wires crossing the thinner wires at right angles—the marks of these wires can be seen in the finished paper if it is held up to the light. "Wove" paper is produced by having a much finer mesh of wires, all of the same diameter, and normally woven in and out of one another like cloth—the wire-marks cannot normally be seen in the finished paper.

Tradition has it that Baskerville invented wove paper, but it is unlikely. Gaskell quoted James Whatman[2] as saying in 1796 that his father

[1] Mores: p. 93.   [2] Gaskell: p. 22.

"first made the wove paper in 1756" but suggests that it must have been much earlier than this. It is strange that although Baskerville's name is always associated with the introduction of wove paper (and it is almost certain that he was the first man to use it in a book) he used it in only three of the books he printed. L. W. Hanson has a very balanced and informative discussion of this whole matter in his review of Gaskell's *Bibliography*.[1] James Wardrop, writing in *Signature* 9 (July 1938) also is certain that Whatman invented wove paper and is almost as certain that he supplied the paper for the Baskerville *Virgil*, "by common consent the first book to be printed on wove paper", although not the whole of the book was printed on wove paper.

The matter of "hot-pressing" is even more obscure. When paper is made by hand in the traditional way, it has a rough surface. This can be made smoother by passing it through hot rollers: "hot-pressing" or "calendering". If done sufficiently, the paper can be given a smooth surface almost like that of vellum.

Yet hand-made paper is so strong and resistant that it has to be dampened before it is printed. This tends to roughen the surface even more, or to reduce the effect of the calendering if this has been done. Baskerville had the idea of hot-pressing his paper after it had been printed: to smooth the paper and, incidentally, to help to set the ink. This latter may well have been suggested by the technique of japanning where the varnish is usually stoved.

That he did this hot-pressing is not in doubt: what has always been contentious is *how* he did it. For example, Lichtenberg in his letter of 1775 says of his visit to Sarah Baskerville:

She makes a secret, however, of the process by which the paper is glazed, though I came much nearer to an explanation of the matter by questions which I put indirectly. She glazed paper for the London booksellers, who stipulate for a particular kind of glaze, for each of which they have their own special names. Thus I have seen paper which only differed slightly from the common variety, and other paper as smooth as a mirror, some sheets of which she gave me. I

---

[1] Hanson: pp. 141–2.

40

enclose a piece of it. Only one young woman and a little girl are needed to tend the machine, and this pair glazes six quires of paper a day. I am almost certain that it is not done by rolling, but in quite an ordinary fashion; namely, that a smooth and very heavy body, whose nature, size, and weight I cannot determine, is passed hither and thither over it, more or less as linen is ironed in Gottingen. I have been assured by a man of learning that the Arabs glazed their paper in a similar way with smoothing-irons of glass. Rollers like yours are instruments intended for pressing together, and glaze only by means of the violence of the pressure, which is really their chief function. I see no reason why one should not carry out by means of one process both pressing and glazing, since the latter can be produced separately, or at least without an excessive expenditure of pressure . . .[1]

Hansard, on the other hand, has a different idea, and is referring to the paper in the books, which is probably not the case with Lichtenberg:

I have been informed recently of a truth at which I have long since guessed, namely that his trade of *japanning book-work* was conducted as follows:—He had a constant succession of hot plates of copper ready, between which, as soon as printed (aye, as they were discharged from the tympan) the sheets were inserted; the wet was thus expelled, the ink set, and the trim glossy surface put on all simultaneously.[2]

There is yet another version in Dreyfus's article in *Signature*:

Although this man, Letellier, had brought over from Birmingham the smoothing press which Baskerville himself had used, when Anisson arrived at Kehl the machine was still dismantled. Letellier would not allow the dismantled parts to be inspected, and told Anisson that he had never seen it in operation in England and had never tried it out since; nevertheless he thought he could achieve the same success with it as Baskerville by following the directions which he had obtained in England. He explained that the machine consisted of two big copper cylinders, just over three feet two inches long and eight and a half inches in diameter. These cylinders were brought into contact not by packing the head of the press with pieces of cardboard (as

[1] M. & Q.: pp. 94–5.   [2] Hansard: p. 311.

happens on a copper-plate press) but by the pressure of screw on the axles of the cylinders. The sheet was fed between these cylinders when it was completely dry, and passed through them only once, although it could do so several times without harm.[1]

However Baskerville glazed or hot-pressed his book-paper, whether by heat alone or by passing it through a machine of his own devising, there can be no doubt at all that he did it, and, while he was experimenting with it, his astute mind saw that this glazed paper had commercial possibilities as writing-paper. This subject is obviously what he and Dodsley were discussing in the two letters last quoted.

In the proposals for printing the poetical works of John Milton, which were issued in 1757, Baskerville gives the names and addresses of booksellers who will take subscriptions for the proposed work. He goes on to say:

And also by *John Baskerville* at his house in *Birmingham. To whom Gentlemen who choose to encourage the undertaking are desired to send their names.* Where the curious in *Writing Paper* may be *furnished* with Superfine post gilt or plain, *glazed* or *unglazed* of his own manufacture, little inferior in smoothness to the finest abortive Vellum. He also sells quarto post gilt and beautifully decorated in the borders at two Shillings and six-pence the quire, octavo ditto at one Shilling and six-pence; and Messages at eight-pence the dozen; and makes large allowance to wholesale dealers.

The paper was still being advertised in *Aris* late in 1765 as available from Mr. Kearsley in Ludgate Street, London, and when Sarah Baskerville was selling up in 1775 the clerk who wrote on her behalf said, "As to Glazing it is an advantageous branch of Business at present in post papers, therefore shu'd make as separate articles but if they choose it it shall be had on very advantageous terms."[2]

Even though Baskerville in his letter to Dodsley in December was talking of printing another "Classick", he already was casting his eyes in

---

[1] Dreyfus: *Signature*, p. 46. [2] see pp. 139–41 for full text.

another direction. On 4th January, 1757, he wrote to a correspondent, who seems to have had good connections although he is not known by name, in the following terms:

Birmingham 4 Jany 1757

Honoured S^r

I have made all the hast in my power to forward to you a Specimen of a common prayer book, as perfect as I can make it. The Size is calculated for people, who begin to want Spectacles but are ashamed to use them at Church.

As you have been pleas'd to treat me with the utmost freedom & good Nature, & have declared yourself no friend to Ceremony: I shall without any; give you an Account of my present Situation. I have pursued the Scheme of printing and Letter founding for Seven Years, with the most intense Application, to the great prejudice of my Eyes, by the daily use of Microscopes, & at the expence of above a thousand pounds, which really makes me short of mony; And tho' I have now brought it to some degree of perfection, & have had very agreeable proofs of the Approbation of the publick; I have no way of refunding the Expense I have been at, without the patronage of the University of Cambridge.

Mr Basket has a Patent for Bibles, Common prayer books & Law books. The Booksellers claim an absolute right in Copys of books, as old as even Milton & Shakespear; the former of which I did design to have printed, but am deterred by Mr Tonson & Co threatening me with a bill in Chancery if I attempt it. My Virgil will be out of the Press about the end of this month, & tho I am happy in having above 500 Subscribers: I consider them as paying a Compliment to the Character & Printing, but fear it will not be to my Advantage to attempt another Classick.

If I find favor with the University, & they give me a Grant to print an Edition of a prayer book according to the Specimen, I would as soon as Virgil was finished & a proper place could be found for their Reception, send to Cambridge two presses, Workmen & all other Requisites, but should be glad to take the Chance of the Edition to my Self, & make the University such Considerations as they should think fit to prescribe. But my highest Ambition is to print a folio Bible, with the same letter of the inclosed Specimen, which would allow a handsom margin, besides Notes, & which I would decorate with a neat black Ornament, between & round the Colums & marginal Notes, about a quarter as broad as the inclos'd Specimen, which may serve to give a rude or imperfect Idea of what I mean & will appear more agreeable to every Eye than the coarse red lines in the best Editions. The Reason of my mentioning a bible at this time is this; that if it was the pleasure of the University to give me a Power to print it, it would be at least twelve months before it could be begun, as it must be printed by Subscription, & about a fourth part of the price advanced as my Capital would not carry it without; the price I imagin would be three & a half or four Guineas in Sheets, everyone of which I would endeavour to make as perfect as the Specimen; it would be two years in the press; I am advancing apace towards old age being now in my fifty second year, & should esteem it a particular happiness to compleat so great a Work before I dye. If I have the honour to have my Specimen handed to the Duke of Newcastle; & its his Grace's pleasure to recommend it to the University, it would I imagin be a means to facilitate the Business. Another Circumstance may possibly be in my Favor, that it may not suit the University to print an Edition of either of the above, whether I did or not. I should be extremely thanful for your Advice, whether it will be proper to address the University by Petition, or in what other manner, or whether my personal application may be dispensed with; as I would by no means be wanting in due honor & respect to the University. I have great hopes & even Expectations of Success from the universal kind Reception I met with at Cambridge; A line from you if there's any Room to flatter my hopes will eternally oblige

Y^r most obed^t hble Servt

John Baskerville

PS. The Specimens are just as they came from the press yesterday, but when finish'd, all the volumes will be as smooth as the black ornament, or the paper I write on.

The rather touching remark (possibly to be seen as having some reference to himself) about the size of the prayerbook is also shrewd. Dibdin, writing about the prayerbooks said:

> *Baskerville* . . . put forth *four* editions of the Book of Common Prayer . . . they are all lovely specimens of press-work; and I cannot bring myself to blame the custom of a most respectable country Squire, in the vicinity of Oxford, who would never read the service and make the responses at church, out of any other edition but that of the *double-columned octavo Baskerville*, nor carry any other devotional Manual with him to the altar than that of the *duodecimo* Baskerville.[1]

Baskerville's eternal optimism about publication is there still in the letter: the *Virgil* did not appear till April. Shenstone, writing on 7th March, says: "My neighbour Baskerville, at the close of this month, publishes his fine edition of Virgil. It will, for *type* & *paper*, be a perfect curiosity. He follows the Cambridge edition . . ."[2]

Yet Dodsley, writing on 7th April, is still waiting for the book:

To Mr Baskerville

Dear Sir

I am very sorry I advertis'd ye Virgil to be publish'd last Month, as you have not enabled me to keep my word with the Public; but I hope it will not be delay'd any longer, as every day you lose now the season is so far advanc'd is certainly a great loss to you. I hope I shall have ye pleasure of seeing you and it together. However, if the delay is occasion'd by your making corrections, I think that a point of so much consequence that no consideration should induce you to publish till it is quite correct. As to the ornamented Paper I will lower the Price since you think it proper, but am still of opinion that it will not sell at our end of the Town, tho' for what reason I cannot imagine. I sent a sortment of it to Bath which is sold, & Mr Loake has sent for a small parcel more; I will send it him at the reduc'd price, & will advertise it to be sold by him also. I shall be glad of twenty Reams of Post made from your own moldes as soon as you can.

---

[1] Dibdin: *Library Companion*, pp. 43–4. [2] Williams CCIV.

I like exceedingly your specimen of a Common Prayer, and hope you are endeavouring to get leave to print one. There is an error in the Exhortation, *shall* for *should*. Your small letter is extreamly beautiful, I wish I could advise what to print with it. What think you of some popular French books? Gilblas, Moliere, or Telemaque? In the Specimen from Melmoth I think you have us'd too many Capitals, which is generally thought to spoil the beauty of printing: but they should never be us'd to adjectives, verbs or adverbs. My best Compliments attend your whole family, and in hopes of seeing you soon

I remain Dear Sir &c

No example of the prayerbook specimen seems to have survived, but the "specimen from Melmoth" is the first of the half dozen type specimens which were published during Baskerville's life and by his widow in the hope of persuading other printers to buy the new type. In this he was unsuccessful: he says in a letter in 1773[1] that he had never sold any types—in that letter, one feels, making a virtue of something that had been forced upon him. But there is some evidence that Baskerville type was acquired by other printers before 1773.

[1] see pp. 130–1 for full text.

3

The *Virgil* finally appeared in April, 1757. It is an astonishing book, as Macaulay implied, and seen after two hundred years, it is still astonishing.

It is difficult to give precedence to its various qualities, but it would be quite wrong not to advance a personal opinion that the most astonishing of its qualities is the press-work and inking. This is surely what marks the book out from its contemporaries: certainly from all the products of the English presses of the time, and even from Foulis. We have become so accustomed to the superb impression of the modern printer, obtained on presses whose pressure and inking can be micrometrically adjusted, that it is only by seeing Baskerville's work against that of his contemporaries that the measure of his skill can really be appreciated.

And one wonders, too, if that skill can ever be fully appreciated by twentieth-century minds. Even if one has used a flat-bed press, inked the type by hand and printed on damped, hand-made paper, one is still taking the advantage that Baskerville did not have of nearly two hundred years of technological improvement.

The simplest example is inking. He or his printers put their ink on the type with leather balls—not a roller made to a tolerance of a minute fraction of an inch. How they managed their standard of inking passes comprehension. To print on damped paper necessitates pushing the type into the paper; and one finishes, as it were, with a little dab of ink of the shape of the letter at the bottom of a depression. Ideally, this depression should not show, or hardly show, on the other side of the paper. If the ink has not been applied to the type with the greatest skill, or if the ink is too runny, it will not be confined to the printing surface of the type but will have overflowed down its side and when the type is pressed into the paper will show on the walls of the depression giving a blurred print. Baskerville managed to get a film of ink on the printing surface of his type and nowhere else; and he used less ink than did most of his contemporaries (Nicholas Boden makes a point of this during the controversy of 1769) and as he continued in his printing career he seems to have used even less—some of the *Virgil* title-pages show rather too much ink. His ink was (and still is) so black that he could afford to do this.

The accuracy of his impression of type on to paper is of the same quality. His hot-pressing after printing would lessen any embossing that his presses did, but even on the pages that have obviously not been hot-pressed (e.g. Pixell's *Songs*), the same splendid, unmistakeable Baskerville superiority is there. However disingenuous it may appear to be to generalise about books which, produced by eighteenth-century methods, must have varied from copy to copy, the fact still remains that any book that he printed is immediately recognisable.

He also used his type only once.[1] Even if this statement made on Sarah's behalf in 1775 is not perfectly true, it is obvious that he never used worn type. And there is a reference in Anisson's report[2] which suggests another reason for the superiority of his printing: "To obtain an edition of 1,500 copies he would print 2000; and from those he would sort out 1,500 of even colour."

He was, of course, an amateur and an auto-didact; and this is probably one of the reasons why he eschewed the methods of contemporary professionals in inking and press-work. But his amateurism, or his ignorance of tradition, or his disregard for the economic facts of a printer's life, does not explain his design and lay-out. The title-page of the *Virgil* is the obvious example, though perhaps not the best. The simplicity of the page—starkness might be a better word—is not original; the Foulis press had used widely spaced capitals before Baskerville. Yet the perfection of the choice of type (Two-line English, French Canon, and Great Primer roman capitals; Double Pica italic capitals), the space between the nine lines, the optical spacing of the capitals, the one word in upper

[1] see p. 140. [2] Dreyfus: *Signature*, p. 48.

PUBLII VIRGILII

MARONIS

BUCOLICA,

GEORGICA,

E T

AENEIS.

BIRMINGHAMIAE:

Typis JOHANNIS BASKERVILLE.

MDCCLVII.

Title-page of the 1757 *Virgil (reduced from 225 × 300 mm)*

and lower case—all these show a sense for design that few men have had in the history of printing from movable type.

Possibly a greater test of a book-designer's skill is a double-page spread in the book: many designers of well-regarded title-pages come to grief if one looks inside their books. Baskerville does not.

If one looks at a double-page spread of the *Virgil*, preferably in the *Aeneid* where there are just two pages of text with no interruptions, there is a superb quality of rightness about it. Most copies have been trimmed by the binders, so that one has to be rather careful about talking of the proportion of the margins. They do not conform to what is now considered the classic proportions, but they are right for the page: he—like all great designers—had an eye.

The page is rather square, and his 30 lines of Great Primer, leaded almost exactly three modern points, sit beautifully on it. The spacing between the lines is completely successful, but the average of five or six points of inter-word space is, by modern perfectionist standards, perhaps a little too much. Yet it would be hyper-critical to complain—as it would be to point out the occasional "river" on the pages.

There are, however, two valid criticisms to be made, one technical, and the other aesthetic. In the *Virgil* (he improved later) the backing-up is by no means perfect; and if the running heads had been set in a smaller size, the pages would have looked better. This latter—the devotion to rather too large-sized type for heads of all kinds—is a feature of all his design.

But the double-page spread still has the air of having been designed, and of having been designed by a man whose feel for the placing of a block of type on to a piece of paper is approaching genius—if one can use such a word in relation to a craft. And he did better later in his career, particularly when he was setting prose.

The "spurious" *Virgil*[1] is typographically almost identical with the genuine 1757 edition. Gaskell discusses it at length and suggests, from the evidence of the paper, that it was probably produced around 1770.[2] It was almost certainly printed to take advantage of the rarity of the 1757

[1] Gaskell 2.
[2] Gaskell: p. 19.

Pp. 205–6 of the 1757 *Virgil* (*reduced from 450 × 300 mm*)

edition by that time. Wm. P. Barlow[1] has suggested that it was produced by Martin during his tenure of the press, but even if this is so, Baskerville must have known about it and condoned its printing.

In July Baskerville was in London, and the acrimony perceptible in Dodsley's letter in April had obviously been forgotten, for "Mr and Mrs Baskerville, Miss Eaves, and Mr Hylton dined with me yesterday" and "they will set out in about ten days or a fortnight . . . and they have persuaded me to accompany them" are extracts from letters Dodsley wrote at the time.

[1] In conversation with the present writer.

51

During the year Baskerville printed one of the few pieces of ephemera which have survived—or which he ever printed. It is a legal document, "Case of the Respondent, Geo. Earl of Shrewsbury . . .",[1] obviously printed after 22nd February 1757 when the case was heard in the Court of Chancery, and before 10th February 1758 when the case was again discussed in the Lords.[2]

The other pieces of non-book printing, apart from specimens of books, or proposals to print books, that Baskerville himself printed are:

1759 "Proposals for a Navigation . . ."[3]
1760 "His Majesty's Most Gracious Speech"[3]
1762 A letter in Latin printed for the University of Cambridge.[4]
1769 "Verses by Boswell"[5]

One can see why Baskerville printed the Cambridge letter: at the time he was closely associated with the University in the printing of the prayerbook. But it is difficult to see why he carried out the other examples of jobbing printing, if these were the only pieces he did. If he had done no jobbing at all, it would have been in keeping with his perfectionist outlook: he was a printer of books and the printing of ephemera was beneath his dignity.

Yet we know that he did turn his hand and his press to the occasional ephemeral piece, and these are so few that one wonders if there are more Baskerville ephemera still waiting to be discovered by someone with a keen eye for type-forms and access to collections of eighteenth-century printing.

After all, the *Shrewsbury Case* was not discovered until the late 1920s (it was first referred to in an article by Graham Pollard in *Fleuron VII*); the Cambridge letter was not recognised as being printed by Baskerville until 1933;[6] *Proposals for a Navigation* was found by Gaskell in the period between the first and second editions of his *Bibliography*, i.e. between 1959 and 1973; and *His Majesty's Speech* came to light only in 1971 when James L. McKelvey wrote in the *Transactions of the Cambridge Biblio-*

[1] Gaskell vi.
[2] Gaskell: pp. 7–8.
[3] Gaskell (2nd ed.) xvii, xviii.
[4] Gaskell xii.
[5] Gaskell xiii.
[6] Gaskell: p. 12.

graphical Society[1] about a letter from Baskerville to the third Earl of Bute which is preserved in the Bute family archives. In the postscript to the letter Baskerville says that he had "printed 1000 of his Majesty's first most gracious Speech".[2] No copy of this is known to have survived. The existence of the *Verses* by Boswell has been known since 1911 at least.[3]

Also in 1757 the "Proposals for Printing by Subscription the Poetical Works of John Milton in Two Volumes" appeared. This was to be printed "for J. & R. Tonson in London".[4] Gaskell has identified at least three versions of the *Proposals* dated 1757, and Straus and Dent mention another, dated 1758. The book did not appear until early in 1759.

It was early in 1758 that, according to Hill, Robert Martin joined Baskerville as a journeyman. He was the son of a local printer. Later he became Baskerville's foreman, took over the press in the 1766–9 period and after printing for Sarah continued on his own account when she gave up the printing business. He died in 1796.

And it was also in 1758 that Baskerville realised one of his chief ambitions. The University of Cambridge decided on 1st December to appoint him Printer to the University:

> Agreed that Mr Baskerville shall have leave to print one Impression of a folio Bible, on a Paper & with a Letter at least as large & good, as the Specimen deliver'd in & signed by him; the Margin to be a little enlarged; & the Ornaments (if any) to be such, as the Syndics shall approve.
>
> Agreed also, that Mr Baskerville shall have leave to print two 8vo Common-Prayer Books of the same size & on as good a Paper and with as good & large a Letter, as the Specimens deliver'd in & signed by him; the Prices to be printed on the Title-Page, & not to be less than six shillings in sheets; & that such leave shall be in force for ten years . . .

The conditions laid down in that part of the agreement were fairly stringent, but it went on to list more: that he was not to print anything else at the University without the permission of the Syndics; that he

[1] Vol. V, pp. 138–41. [2] see p. 82.
[3] Hanson: p. 138. [4] Gaskell vii.

could not describe himself as Printer to the University on books printed elsewhere than at the University; that his printing-office was to be open at all times for inspection by the Syndics' representatives; that he could not take away any books without notice sufficient to allow the number of books to be inspected; that he had to pay the University £20 for every 1000 8vo prayerbooks he printed; that he had to offer sufficient security to indemnify the University from any prosecution which might result from his printing.

Baskerville agreed to the conditions, and on 17th December he and John Eaves gave security for £500 each.

The following month he announced his appointment in *Aris* of 22nd January, 1759:

> John Baskerville begs Leave to inform the Publick, that he has lately obtained from the University of Cambridge, full Powers to print, under their Privilege, Octavo Common-Prayer-Books on a large fine Royal Paper, and Letter of two Sizes, (to wit) Great Primer in long lines, and English in columns, and one Edition of a Folio Bible; the former of which Prayer-Books he hopes to have ready for Publication about *Midsummer* next; the other with all convenient Speed. The Bible will be published by Subscription, at Four Guineas in Sheets: A Specimen, with Proposals, will be ready in about two months. No Care or Expense will be spared in making the three Books as correct and elegant as possible.—Those Gentlemen who are inclined to encourage his Undertakings, are desired to give him a Line, signifying their Pleasure, and the Favour will be most gratefully acknowledg'd
>
> By their most obedient humble Servant
> John Baskerville
>
> N.B. A Book-binder, who is a good Hand, may have constant Employment.

This appeared as the second part of the advertisement about the publication of the Milton.[1]

In view of the date of the Cambridge decision, one must assume that Carlyle, who visited Baskerville in May 1758, and said "Baskerville was

[1] see p. 60.

on hands with his folio Bible at this time . . ."[1] confused the preparation of the "Specimen" referred to in the agreement with Cambridge with the printing of the Bible itself.

Yet before he did anything about his prospectuses for the prayerbooks or the Bible, or even the *Milton*, he produced another book: *Avon, A Poem in Three Parts*.[2] It was written by John Huckell and sold by Dodsley. Huckell was a clergyman, living in Isleworth, Middlesex, but he had been born and brought up in Stratford-on-Avon.

Avon is not among Baskerville's masterpieces. The pages have too much interlinear space and, in the one copy seen, the "O" in "Poem" on the title-page was inverted. It has all the signs of a job hastily done— possibly to clear the presses for more important work.

That book was published in early June 1758, and in the same month another of Baskerville's plans came to fruition. He obviously had not been content with his negotiations at Cambridge and must also have been in contact with Oxford—in this case with a rather more limited and unusual suggestion. On 6th June, 1758, the Delegates of the Oxford University Press ordered:

> that this Delegacy will at their next meeting take into consideration Mr Baskerville's proposals for casting a set of new Greek types

and on 5th July, ordered:

> Dr Blackstone to be empowered to agree with John Baskerville to make a new set of Greek punches, matrices and moulds in Great Primer for the use of the University and to cast 3 cwt of type @ 200 guineas for the whole.

On 31st January 1759, the Delegates gave Mr Musgrave leave to print his *Euripides* at the University Press in John Baskerville's types as soon as they arrived, and on 11th March they ordered:

> That a Greek Testament in Quarto and Octavo be printed in Baskerville's letter, and three or four Gentlemen of Learning and Accuracy be desired separately to correct the Proofs.

[1] Carlyle: p. 369.   [2] Gaskell 3.

The type was delivered in 1761 and on 23rd June the Delegates ordered 500 copies in Quarto and 2,000 in Octavo to be printed. The books appeared in 1763.[1]

The books, and the type, had a mixed reception, even though the *St James Chronicle* of 5th September, 1758 (quoted by Nichols[2]) had said: "It is not doubted but that ingenious artist will excel in that character, as he has already done in the Roman and Italic, in his elegant edition of Virgil." Mores has no doubts on the subject at all:

> *Mr Baskerville* of *Birmingham*, that enterprizing place, made some attempts at *letter-cutting*, but desisted with good reason. the Greek cut by him or *his* for the Univ. of Oxf. is execrable, indeed he can hardly claim a place amongst the *letter-cutters* . . .[3]

Dibdin called them "these beautiful editions," and said, "The type which is without contractions, is large and distinct; and in both editions has an elegant effect."[4] Whereas Reed said, "The letter is neat, but stiff and cramped, and apparently formed on an arbitrary estimate of conventional taste, and without any reference to any accepted model."[5]

To the eye of the present writer, who has no expertise in the assessment of exotics, Baskerville's Greek seems very acceptable. The obvious comparison is with the Greek which Alexander Wilson cut for the Foulis Brothers a few years before Baskerville cut his. Some of Baskerville's letters, individually, seem more pleasing than Wilson's, but the impression given when one compares a page of Baskerville with a page of Wilson is that Wilson is the better. Baskerville's is a neat letter, but it is true that it has a slightly cramped, or condensed quality about it (very strange when one thinks of the roman letter), and it is rather stiff and spidery. Wilson's letters seem almost to flow along the line. Yet one wonders if the comparison is fair: the Oxford *Testament* is not a distinguished book, and the *Homer* is among the best the Foulis Press produced.

In the summer of 1758, Benjamin Franklin came to Birmingham and met Baskerville. He came to the city bearing a letter of introduction to

[1] Gaskell Add 1 and 2.
[2] Nichols: *Lit. Anec.* III, p. 451.
[3] Mores: p. 81.
[4] Dibdin: *Classics* I, p. 157.
[5] TBR: p. 54.

The greek punches cut in 1758–61 for the University of Oxford. The book shown is the New Testament, printed at Oxford in 1763

Matthew Boulton from John Michell of Cambridge, one of the most distinguished scientists of the day, but he obviously took the opportunity of also making Baskerville's acquaintance. Franklin was at this time senior partner in a printing firm at Philadelphia and would certainly have been interested in Baskerville's activities. He knew of them, for he had subscribed for six copies of the *Virgil*; and when he was in Birmingham he bought a selection of Baskerville's japanned goods for which he paid £2. 4s.[1] This meeting was the beginning of a friendship and fairly regular exchange of letters which continued to the end of Baskerville's life.

Franklin was generous with his copies of the *Virgil*. The bill for binding them appears in his notes of his expenditure, and he presented one of them to Harvard: "I beg the College will do me the favour to accept a Virgil I send in the Case, thought to be the most curiously printed of any Book hitherto done in the World."[2] The book is still at Harvard.

At least two other copies were commented on by Franklin's friends; and one, sent to Isaac Norris, brought forth a request to Franklin to enter him as a subscriber to any classics which Baskerville might produce in the future: "that I may have an Opportunity of contributing my Mite to encourage such a curious and Ingenious Man . . ."[3] Franklin took him at his word and Norris appears in the list of subscribers to the *Milton*: "Isaac Norris, Speaker of the Assembly of Pennsylvania."

In August and September of the same year (1758) there was a slight coolness in the friendship between Shenstone and Baskerville, in which Matthew Boulton was involved. The poet must have written some verses derogatory to Baskerville and sent them to Boulton on 23rd August:

> The enclosed Impromptu may amuse Mr Boulton for a moment; but he must give me his word & honour y[t] he will make no other use of it, before I see Him.

Baskerville must somehow have become aware of the verse, possibly through a Joseph Giles, an engraver, who is mentioned in a later letter, for Shenstone wrote again to Boulton on 18th September:

[1] Franklin: Vol 9, pp. 258–9. [2] Franklin: Vol 8, p. 53.
[3] Franklin: Vol 8, p. 80.

Finally I could wish, y^t Mr. Baskerville would not be so extremely idle as to give a Construction to this Trifle, which cannot possibly be countenanc'd by any *one* Consideration . . .

And when he wrote again a week later, 25th September, the affair seems to be coming to an end:

> . . . I hope y^t Mr Baskerville has by this time been induc'd to construe y^t idle ballad according to ye sense that was obviously intended; & y^t I shall have no further occasion to say anything on that subject.
> I have receiv'd ye 2 copies I gave to Mr B^n. and Mr Giles. Had I given copies to Mr Baskerville's enemies, ye case had been very different . . .[1]

Whether the coolness between Baskerville and Shenstone was serious or not, it certainly did not interfere with business relations between Baskerville and Boulton. There is in the collection at the Birmingham Assay Office a receipted bill which shows that the business transacted between them at this time covered an extraordinarily miscellaneous area:

Mr Matthew Boulton to J. Baskerville

		D^r		C^r	
25 Sept^r '58	To 1 ream of Paper	– 10 –	By Mr Tottie Cash	4. 18. 6	
	To d^o. cut in Cards	– 12 –			
8 Nov^r	To a Mare sold 10. 10. –		Ballance	14. 11. 6	
	To 1 Avon	3. –			
	To Mr Baily's Draft 6.	3. –			
	To 32 Puncheons 1.	12. –			
	£19. 10 –			£19. 10. 0	

Rec^d the contents in full

John Baskerville

By November, Baskerville must no longer have had any ill-feeling left towards Shenstone, for the latter, writing to Thomas Percy (who received the letter on 1st December, 1758) said:

> . . . Possibly I may be one day tempted to furnish out a small Miscellany; having a press in my own *Neighbourhood*, so very favorable to my

[1] Williams CCXXIV–VI.

Indolence . . . Baskerville's Milton, they tell me comes out in ye Xt^mas holidays . . .[1]

unless, of course, the last sentence suggests that he was not in personal touch with Baskerville. On 6th January, 1759, he refers again to the projected *Miscellany* in a letter to Richard Jago.[2]

The *Milton*[3] appeared a little later than Shenstone had forecast. Straus and Dent give the actual date as 27th January, 1759 and *Aris* of Monday, 22nd January, 1759 carried an advertisement:

> On Saturday the 27th Instant will be Published. Milton's Poetical Works, in Two Volumes, Octavo, Royal Paper, printed by John Baskerville at Birmingham; who returns Thanks to those Gentlemens and Ladies who have favour'd him with Their Names; and desires they would take up their Volumes of any of the following Book-sellers: Messieurs *Dodsley* in *Pall-Mall*, Mr. *Tonson* in the *Strand*, Mr. *Pote* in *Fleet-Street*, Mr. *Stuart* in *Pater-Noster-Row*, Mr. *Dell* in *Great Tower Street, London* or of *John Baskerville* at *Birmingham*; who takes this Opportunity of acknowledging, a second Time, the Favour of Mr. Tonson, who on being informed some Hundred Copies were sub-scrib'd for more than printed, (tho' the Number was 1500) has given him leave to print a Second Edition of 700 Sets more, which will be published soon after Midsummer, on a very large fine Paper, at One Guinea in Sheets. Gentlemen who shall take the Small Paper, may exchange for the Large, on paying the Difference to any of the Trade above . . .

The following week the same advertisement appeared, but this time headed, "On Saturday was published . . ."

The *Milton* is rather disappointing after the *Virgil*: the octavo looks rather cramped; the quarto is better. Hansard certainly liked it:

> There is an edition of Milton's Paradise Lost, "Birmingham: printed by John Baskerville, for J. & R. Tonson, in London M.DCC.LIX." (4to) now before me, most admirably printed. The type (pica) is

[1] Williams CCXXX.   [2] Williams CCXXXIII.
[3] Gaskell 4 and 5.

manifestly an improvement upon the "slender and delicate" mentioned by Mr Dibdin; I should think it, on the contrary, approaching to the *embonpoint*, and admirably calculated, by extending the size (if in exact proportion), for works of the largest dimensions. The italic possesses much room for admiration. The ink and press-work are beautifully clear and uniform,—a scrutinising look throughout the volume has been unable to discover any one page of a shade different in colour from another. The paper is very fine, all rag, no cotton, no bleach, no plaster, not machine-made: it is thick, rather yellow, compared to what is doctored up in the present day, and of the description called wove.[1]

In the preface to the *Milton* Baskerville wrote over his own name the only real statement of his aims and purpose he ever made:

Amongst the several mechanic Arts that have engaged my attention, there is no one which I have pursued with so much steadiness and pleasure, as that of *Letter-Founding*. Having been an early admirer of the beauty of Letters, I became insensibly desirous of contributing to the perfection of them. I formed to my self Ideas of greater accuracy than had yet appeared, and have endeavoured to produce a *Sett* of *Types* according to what I conceived to be their true proportion.

Mr. *Caslon* is an Artist to whom the Republic of Learning has great obligations; his ingenuity has left a fairer copy for my emulation, than any other master. In his great variety of *Characters* I intend not to follow him; the Roman and Italic are all I have hitherto attempted; if in these he has left room for improvement, it is probably more owing to that variety which divided his attention, than to any other cause. I honor his merit, and only wish to derive some small share of Reputation, from an Art which proves accidentally to have been the object of our mutual pursuit.

After having spent many years, and not a little of my fortune in my endeavours to advance this art; I must own it gives me great Satisfaction, to find that my Edition of *Virgil* has been so favorably received. The improvement in the Manufacture of the *Paper*, the *Colour*,

[1] Hansard: pp. 310–11.

and *Firmness* of the *Ink* were not overlooked; nor did the accuracy of the workmanship in general, pass unregarded. If the judicious found some imperfections in the *first attempt*, I hope the present work will shew that a proper use has been made of their Criticisms: I am conscious of this at least, that I received them as I ever shall, with that degree of deference which every private man owes to the Opinion of the public.

It is not my desire to print many books; but such only, as are *books* of *Consequence*, of *intrinsic merit*, or *established Reputation*, and which the public may be pleased to see in an elegant dress, and to purchase at such a price, as will repay the extraordinary care and expense that must necessarily be bestowed upon them. Hence I was desirous of making an experiment upon some one of our best English Authors, among those *Milton* appeared the most eligible. And I embrace with pleasure the opportunity of acknowledging in this public manner the generosity of *Mr. Tonson*; who with singular politeness complimented me with the privilege of printing an entire Edition of that *Writers Poetical Works*.

In the execution of this design, if I have followed with exactness the Text of *Dr. Newton*, it is all the merit of *that* kind which I pretend to claim. But if this performance shall appear to persons of judgment and penetration, in the *Paper, Letter, Ink* and *Workmanship* to excel; I hope their approbation may contribute to procure for me what would indeed be the extent of my Ambition, a power to print an *Octavo Common-Prayer Book*, and a FOLIO BIBLE.

Should it be my good fortune to meet with this indulgence, I wou'd use my utmost efforts to perfect an Edition of them with the greatest Elegance and Correctness; a work which I hope might do some honor to the English Press, and contribute to improve the pleasure, which men of true taste will always have in the perusal of those *sacred Volumes*.

JOHN BASKERVILLE

A second edition of the quarto *Milton* was issued later in 1759[1], but

[1] Gaskell 6 and 7.

Tonson, or Baskerville, seems to have over-estimated the demand for it. In 1768 *Aris* of 15th August carried an advertisement:

T. Davies, in Russel-Street, Covent Garden, having purchased the following books, late the property of Jacob Tonson, Esq. &c. proposes to sell them at the following prices:

... Paradise Lost and Regained, printed by Baskerville, 2 vols, 4to, 1l. 8s. ...

4

✳◇✳◇✳◇✳◇✳◇✳◇✳◇✳◇✳◇✳◇✳◇✳◇✳◇✳◇✳

Having seen the *Milton* successfully through the press and published, Baskerville began to concentrate on his Cambridge venture. By the end of May he appears to have completed most of the arrangements, for he wrote to the Vice-Chancellor on 31st May, 1759:

Sʳ,

  I have at last sent everything requisite to begin the prayer book at Cambridge. The bearer, Mʳ. Thos. Warren, is my deputy in conducting the whole. I have ordered him to inform you of every step he takes and to desire you would appoint a person to tell out the number of sheets before they go to press, and again before they are packed up for Birmingham. Mʳ Bentham will inform you how many sheets per thousand are ordered for wast. I have attempted several other ornaments but none of them please me so well as the specimen, which I hope will be approved by you and the gentlemen of the Syndick. I propose printing off 2000 the first impression but only 1000 of the State Holidays &c. which the patentee has left out. The paper is very good and stands me in 27 or 28 shillings the ream.

  I am taking great pains in order to produce a striking title page and specimen of the Bible, which I hope will be ready in about six weeks. The importance of the work demands all my attention, not only for my own (eternal) reputation; but (I hope) also to convince the world, that the university in the honour done me has not entirely misplaced their favours.

  You will please to accept, and give my most respectful duty to the

64

University, particularly to the gentlemen of the Syndick. I should be very happy if I could make an interest to a few gent[n] to whom the work would not be disagreeable to survey the sheets, after my people had corrected them as accurately as they are able, that I might, if possible, be free from every error of the press; for which I would gladly make a suitable acknowledgment.

I procured a sealed copy of the Common Prayer with much trouble and expense from the Cathedral of Litchfield, but found it the most inaccurate and ill printed work I ever saw so that I returned it with thanks.

I am &c.

John Baskerville.

Whether he produced the Bible specimen in the six weeks he hoped, it is impossible to know, but during the summer the press must have been occupied for some of the time in printing the letterpress for John Pixell's *Songs*, which was published by October, 1759. Straus and Dent had doubts about this book;[1] Gaskell accepts it.[2] Pixell was Vicar of Edgbaston from 1750 to 1784, and a friend of Shenstone's to whom the first song is dedicated. The title is *A Collection of Songs . . . Set to Musick by Mr. Pixell . . .* and it merely bears the information, "Birmingham, Printed for the Author . . ."

The book would not have taken much time for Baskerville to produce: only the title-page and the pages of the list of subscribers are printed from type. The rest of the book consists of forty-one pages of engraved words and music, signed "Engrav'd and Printed by M. Broome in Birmingham". There can be little doubt of the authenticity of the letterpress printing of the book; and it has one or two interesting features: the first use, on the title-page, of Baskerville's lozenge and star ornament in a book; his rare swash capital "M" in "Mr. Pixell"; and the paper, which seems not to have been hot-pressed.

Among all the other activities going on during the summer of 1759, Dodsley was staying at the Leasowes with Shenstone, preparing his edition of the *Fables*,[3] and it is most unlikely that he did this without some visits to Easy Hill.

[1] S. & D.: p. 32, note 1. [2] Gaskell 8. [3] Williams: p. 519 note.

The first variant of the Specimen and Proposals for the Bible may not have been produced in the six weeks after Baskerville's letter to the Vice-Chancellor, but it bears the date 1759. The second is dated 1st January, 1760, and the only other change is in the list of booksellers.[1]

There is a cryptic reference to this specimen in one of Shenstone's letters to Thomas Percy early in 1760: "I think entirely with Mr. P. with regard to Baskerville's bible—& mention'd ye same to Him long ago";[2] and at the foot of an advertisement in *Aris* dated Monday, 4th May, 1761 there is a note:

> N. B. J. Baskerville will publish soon a new Specimen of his intended Folio Bible, quite plain, with the Marginal Notes at the Bottom of the Pages, as many have objected to his ornamented Specimen; . . .

Hanson draws attention to a similar advertisement in the *London Chronicle* of 11th April, 1761.[3]

The third variant[4] is dated 1st August, 1761, and there are considerable changes, mainly in the design—but also in the conditions. The 1759 set of Proposals were:

I. As the University of Cambridge has done Mr Baskerville the honour to elect him one of their Printers; this work will be printed there in one Volume Folio, with the same Paper and Letter as this Specimen.

II. The Price to Subscribers will be four Guineas in Sheets; one half to be paid at the time of subscribing; and the other at the delivery of the perfect Book.

III. It will be put to Press with all possible Expedition, and delivered to Subscribers in three Years from the date of these Proposals.

IV. Some will be printed with an Ornament, like the first Page of this Specimen, and some with plain lines, like the second; the Subscribers are desired to mention at the time of subscribing, which sort they choose.

[1] Gaskell viii.
[2] Williams CCLVII.
[3] Hanson: p. 139.
[4] The only known copy is in the collection of Wm. P. Barlow.

V. After the Subscription is closed, the Price will be raised.

VI. Those who subscribe for Six shall have a Seventh gratis.

And these were followed by an address "To the Publick", saying why a subscription was necessary, and an "Advertisement" mentioning the prayerbooks, the *Milton* and the forthcoming *Juvenal & Persius*.

In the 1761 Proposal, Baskerville did not ask for his four guineas till the Bible was completed; he promised delivery by the end of 1762; and he said:

IV. As many Gentlemen have objected to every Kind of Ornament round the Page, the Work will be printed quite plain, with the marginal Notes all at the Bottom, according to the annexed Specimen.

The address to the public was hardly changed; the Advertisement mentioned only the *Milton* and the *Juvenal*.

There are some minor changes in the lay-out of the title-pages in the two sets of proposals (confined to the last three lines) but the specimen text-pages have changed completely.

In the spring of 1760 appeared *Edwin and Emma* by David Mallet, a sixteen-page quarto, printed for A. Millar in the Strand,[1] and in May there was a reprint of the octavo *Milton*.[2] Some time during the year Baskerville also produced a type specimen.[3]

It was in 1760, too, that Baskerville received a letter from Benjamin Franklin, who paid him a visit in late September. The actual date of the letter is uncertain as the original is lost; but it was most probably sent late in 1760 after Franklin returned to London following his trip to Coventry, Worcester and Birmingham.

Baskerville used an extract from the letter as an "unsolicited testimonial" at the foot of the advertisements which he inserted at the beginning of August, 1763, in various London newspapers to announce the publication of his Bible:

[1] Gaskell 11.
[2] Gaskell 9, 10.
[3] Gaskell ix.

Extract of a Letter from Benjamin Franklin, Esq; to J. Baskerville.

Craven-street, London.

Dear Sir,

Let me give you a pleasant Instance of the Prejudice some have entertained against your Work. Soon after I returned, discoursing with a Gentleman concerning the Artists of Birmingham, he said you would be a Means of blinding all the Readers in the Nation; for the Strokes of your Letters, being too thin and narrow, hurt the Eye, and he could never read a Line of them without Pain. I thought, said I, you were going to complain of the Gloss on the Paper, some object to. No, no, says he, I have heard that mentioned; but it is not that—it is in the Form and Cut of the Letters themselves: They have not that natural and easy Proportion between the Height and Thickness of the Stroke which makes the common Printing so much the more comfortable to the Eye.—You see this Gentleman was a Connoisseur. In vain I endeavoured to support your Character against the Charge: He knew what he felt, and could see the Reason of it, and several other Gentlemen among his Friends had made the same Observation, &c.—Yesterday he called to visit me, when, mischievously bent to try his Judgment, I stept into my Closet, tore off the top of Mr. Caslon's Specimen, and produced it to him as yours brought with me from Birmingham, saying, I had been examining it since he spoke to me, and could not for my Life perceive the Disproportion he mentioned, desiring him to point it out to me. He readily undertook it, and went over the several Founts, showing me every where what he thought Instances of that Disproportion; and declared, that he could not then read the Specimen without feeling very strongly the Pain he had mentioned to me. I spared him that Time the Confusion of being told, that these were the Types he had been reading all his Life with so much Ease to his Eyes; the Types his adored Newton is printed with, on which he has pored not a little; nay, the very Types his own Book is printed with, for he is himself an Author, and yet never discovered this painful Disproportion in them, till he thought they were yours.

I am, &c.

In spite of the malicious pleasure Baskerville must have felt on reading this, there can be little doubt that the event in 1760 which must have given him most pleasure (though subsequently he seems to have had doubts about it; and he certainly had troubles with it) was the publication of his octavo prayerbook.[1]

Gaskell dates the publication of the first edition as before 4th July, 1760,[2] and *Aris* gives the actual publication day as 19th May, 1760, in the following advertisement:

> . . . *On Monday the 19th May, will also be published, Price 6s. 6d. in Quires,* A large COMMON PRAYER BOOK, in One Volume Octavo, Royal Paper, long lines, printed at Cambridge by John Baskerville, Printer to the University, for which the Trade in London, are desired to apply to Mr Dod . . .

There are considerable variations in the prayerbooks;[3] a second edition appeared later in the year (after 25th October) and a third edition in 1762.[4] A duodecimo version was also published in 1762.[5]

The position is probably best summarised by Townsend and Currier:[6]

> . . . Baskerville printed his Book of Common Prayer under the auspices of Cambridge University. He planned two editions, one to be printed in the customary long lines, the other in double columns; and he printed both editions with and without ornamental borders. The first copies were issued in 1760, but on October 25th of that year occurred the death of King George II. George, Prince of Wales, succeeded to the throne. These events necessitated a change in the prayers for the royal family, and the leaves containing these prayers were cancelled and new ones printed. Also, the price of the volume was twice increased, and since the original price of 6s. 6d. was given on the title page, new title pages were printed and the old ones cancelled. As a result of these changes there were issued a confusing number of combinations of cancelled and uncancelled leaves, and old and new title pages in copies with single or double columns, with

[1] Gaskell 12.   [2] Gaskell: p. 30 note.   [3] Gaskell: p. 30.
[4] Gaskell 13, 19.   [5] Gaskell 20.   [6] T. & C.: p. 286.

or without borders. Out . . . of thirty-three Prayer Books, we have distinguished sixteen different editions, issues or variants . . .

Poor Baskerville! His advertisement in *Aris* of Monday, 29th December, 1760, really shows how things were crowding in on him. He advertises a new edition of the prayerbook in columns, mentions his edition in long lines, apologises for increasing the price, says he has the specimen and proposals for the Bible available, that he has the *Juvenal* in the press, and that there are a few sets of *Milton* still unsold.

According to a statement in Nichols,[1] Baskerville in 1764 "had the honour of presenting to His Majesty, and to the Princess Dowager of Wales, his then newly printed Octavo Common Prayer Book; which was most gracefully received"; but it is likely that Shenstone is the more accurate when he wrote, in 1761, on 1st March: "My Lord Dartmouth has undertaken to present two to the King & Princess . . ."[2]

In view of Baskerville's statement in the letter he wrote in 1773[3] to the President of the Académie des Sciences where he said that he had never sold any type, a rather strange event took place on Monday, 24th November, 1760. *Aris's Birmingham Gazette* appeared with a re-set masthead, or title-piece as it is now called. The full title of the paper at that time was *Aris's Birmingham Gazette; or The General Correspondent* and in this issue this title was set in Baskerville's French Canon type.

The paper continued to use this type for its title (although no other Baskerville type appears anywhere else in the paper) until March, 1767, although in March 1763 it dropped the second part of its title and became simply *Aris's Birmingham Gazette*. The issue dated Monday, 30th March, 1767 has this title set in a large size of what looks very much like a Caslon type and it continued to use this for many years.

The next book Baskerville was to print was Dodsley's *Fables*. It had been in preparation for at least twelve months[4] and on 7th July 1760 Shenstone, in a letter to the Rev. R. Graves, mentions the fact that Dodsley was to come to the Leasowes "in about a fortnight, and prints *one* edition of his Fables by means of Baskerville's press and paper".[5] For

---

[1] Nichols: *Lit. Anec.* III, p. 452.   [2] Williams CCLXIX.
[3] see p. 131.   [4] see p. 65.   [5] Williams CCLXII.

ARIS's Birmingham GAZETTE,
OR,
The General Correspondent.

Price Two-pence Halfpenny. MONDAY, AUGUST 30, 1762. VOL. XXI. No. 1084.

Thursday's Post.

Since our last arrived a Mail from Holland.

P E T E R S B U R G H, (Russia) July 19. The following is an Extract from the Journal of the Proceedings of the Senate, of the 18th.

THE Chevalier de Panin reported to the Senate, that the Empress having resolved to go to see the Corpse of the late Emperor Peter III. and afterwards to assist at his Funeral, he was apprehensive that the Shock would be too much for her tender Heart, and that she would abandon herself to excess of Grief, the rather as she had wept incessantly ever since she heard of his Death; and that he and the Hetman Count Rasomowsky had endeavoured to divert her from her Resolution; but without Effect; whereupon the Senate, fearing some fatal Alteration in her Imperial Majesty's Health, waited upon her in a Body, to beseech her to change her Purposes. At last, but not without Regret, she yielded to their humble Representations, which was notified to the Senate by the Attorney-General.'

BERLIN, (Germany) August 7. The Baron de Munchausen, Counsellor of State, and President of the Regency of Hanover, arrived here a few Days ago. After-having had several Conferences with the Count de Finckenstein, Minister of State for the foreign Department, he set out Yesterday for Silesia, in order to acquit himself of a Commission with his Majesty. The Object of his Commission is not known; but some People think that it relates to some new Overtures for reconciling Matters between this Court and that of Vienna: Others imagine that it relates to some Measure that have been concerted for bringing the new Sovereign of Russia to a proper Way of Thinking; but this is mere Conjecture.

From the Army of the Prince of Conde at Grunberg, Aug. 9.
Yesterday Col. de Wurmser went with his Regiment of Light Troops to reconnoitre the Castle of Ulrickstein, occupied

neral Stainville. The Prince of Conde, by the last Advices, was still at Grenberg. He had endeavoured to force the Post of Hombourg upon the Ohme, in which he failed; as he likewise did in an Attempt upon the Left of the Hereditary Prince's Corps at Ranrod, on the 9th, at that Time commanded by Lieutenant General Hardenberg. The Hereditary Prince is since returned to his Corps from the main Army, and intended to march forward on the 13th Instant.

It is said, that the Trenches were opened before Almeyda on the 25th of July; and the Letters add, that the Spanish Troops are in great Want of Quarters & Refreshment.

L O N D O N, August 24.

ADMIRALTY-OFFICE, August 24. His Majesty's Ship Liverpool commanded by Captain Richard Knight, sailed the 27th of last Month from Plymouth on a Cruise; and the same Day fell in with and took Le Jacques, a French Privateer, of two Carriage and eight Swivel Guns, with Forty-one Men, from Roscow. And on the 18th Instant, in the Latitude 49.35. Capt. Knight retook the Two Brothers, bound from Carolina for London with Rice. *Ibus far Lond.Gaz.*

By Letters from Constantinople of the 3d ult. we have an Account that the Plague raged at Aleppo and Alexandretta, insomuch that Two-fifths at least of the Inhabitants of the last City had been already carried off by that terrible Scourge; and Adana, a City of Natolia, was equally afflicted.

According to Letters from Hamburgh of the 13th Inst. the Empress of Russia had assured the King of Denmark, that she designed to live in good Harmony and Friendship with him; but would not give up the just Claim the late Emperor her Consort had to Part of the Danish Holstein, which would be demanded of him as soon as her Son Prince Paul Petrowitz is of Age.

By express Order of the Empress of Russia, the Russian Troops are hastening their March homewards as much as possible. Part of them are expected to arrive in Livonia by the End of this Month.

The Chief Engineer at Schweidnitz, who was formerly in the French Service, has declared that he expects to be able to maintain the Siege for two Months. It is generally thought in the Prussian Army, that Marshal Daun will make some Attempt to save that Place, which is of such great Importance to the Empress-Queen.

At the late Sale of the Russian Magazines at Colberg, some Austrians, Agents for the Court of Vienna, exerted themselves

Express at New-York in 15 Days from the Havannah, with Advice that Lord Albemarle landed the Forces at the Havannah, the 15th of June, after a very warm Reception; but after some Time, they repulsed the Spaniards with great Loss of the latter; that they had made themselves Masters of the Heights which commanded the Harbour, and had almost destroyed Morro's Castle. There is likewise an Account, that the Crew belonging to a Privateer, and a Party of Rangers, landed on an Island near the Havannah, in order to get some fresh Provisions, and were surrounded by a Party of Spaniards, who, after the English had laid down their Arms, killed the greatest Part of them, and cut off both the Ears of the Lieutenant belonging to the Rangers, and slit up his Nose, and then sent him back to Lord Albemarle to tell his Lordship that they would serve all the English in the same Manner as they had done him and his Companions, whenever they fell into their Hands; to which his Lordship returned for Answer, that he would neither give nor take Quarter, but would put all the Spaniards to the Sword.

Yesterday arrived in the River the Hermione.

By the Accounts received from Madrid of the Treasure, &c. on board the Hermione, her Cargo appears to be worth 1,300,000l. Sterling;

Saturday a fifth Box of Gold was found at the Bank, which makes 45,000l. difference to the Captors.

On Saturday last Six Women, who are Wives of Six Seamen belonging to the Active, that took the Hermione, had a Dinner at Greenwich; after which they went into a Landau, with three Children, three Sailors behind with a Flag, one in the Boot, two on the Top, and a Fidler in the Center, and made a Parade through the Town.

Yesterday at Noon the Right Hon. the Earl of Buckinghamshire set out from his House in Dover-Street for Gravesend, to embark there on board the Portland Man of War for Peterburgh.

Her Majesty and the Prince of Wales are so well, that the Drums beat and the Musick plays again when Guard is relieved at St. James's.

All Persons of Fashion are admitted to see the Royal Infant, under the following Restrictions, viz. that in passing through the Apartments they step with the greatest Caution, to avoid disturbing his Highness; and that they do not offer to touch him. For greater Security also, in this last Respect, a Part of the Apartment is latticed off in the Chinese Manner, to prevent curious Persons from approaching too close.

Title-piece of Aris's Birmingham Gazette, the title set in Baskerville's French Canon type (reduced)

the rest of that year, Shenstone is constantly referring to the printing of the book: on 11th August he refers to Dodsley residing with him for nearly two months to correct the edition of the Fables and says that the book will surpass *Prolusions*;[1] and on 1st October says that "Dodsley is gone to spurr Baskerville . . . I believe Dodsley's Fables will be printed off in about a Fortnight . . ."[2] But on 10th November (and how familiar the story is) "Mr Dodsley's Fables are not quite printed off here, thro some Mistakes yt have occasioned ye loss of three or four reams of Paper—However wn fresh Paper arrives, they will be finished in 3 days time . . .".[3]

The book[4] was published on or about 9th February 1761, according to *Aris*:

This Day are Published, Price bound 5s.
Printed by Mr. Baskerville, on a superfine Paper, and adorned with Copper-Plates, designed by Wale, and engraved by Grignion, Select Fables of Aesop, and other Fabulists. In Three Books.
I. Fables from the Ancients
II. Fables from the Moderns.
III. Fables newly invented
To which are prefixed, the Life of Aesop, and an Essay on Fable by R. Dodsley
* *   Also a smaller Edition, for the Use of Schools, adorned with the
  *   same Copper-Plates, Price Three shillings.
        Printed for R. and J. Dodsley in Pall-Mall; and sold by M. Cooper in Pater-Noster-Row.

It was the first of Baskerville's books to be issued with illustrations, although some copies of his *Virgil*, and of the *Milton*, are found with plates inserted. Shenstone says he "procured a copy of the Fables from Mr Baskerville, *before* the Cutts *were inserted*, & have by the help of Mr Alcock (a Painter) supplied the places of the *emblematick* prints with some devices of my own . . ."[5]

[1] Williams CCLXIII; and on p. 560 (note 6) "Prolusions or Select Pieces of Antient Poetry . . .", published by Tonson, 1760, for Edward Capell.
[2] Williams CCLXIV.   [3] Williams CCLXV.
[4] Gaskell 14.   [5] Williams CCLXVII.

The book must have been a success for on 2nd May, 1761 (less than three months after publication) Shenstone informed the Rev. R. Graves:

> ... Mr. Dodsley had sold two thousand of his Fables long ago; but complained that he should *lose* thirty pounds by my neighbour Baskerville's impression and that he should not be more than ten pounds gainer, upon the whole. I told him it was enough, in books of *this sort*, if the first edition paved the way for future establishment in schools ... I would *wish* him to give the polite world one more edition from Baskerville's press.[1]

However much Dodsley lost on the Baskerville version of the *Fables*, he had a second edition printed in 1764, although the book may not have been published before 1766.[2]

The autumn of 1760 must have been fairly trying, with Shenstone and Dodsley constantly visiting him; and it is not surprising that the next book to appear from the press was one Baskerville printed for publication by himself: another edition of a classic text. He had announced his intention of printing the satires of Juvenal and Persius in his specimen and proposals for the Bible in 1759 and 1760, and in various of the advertisements for other books. It was published in May 1761.[3] *Aris* of Monday, 4th May, carried the following advertisement:

> This day were published
> In one elegant Volume in Quarto Royal, price 12s in Sheets
> JUVENAL and PERSIUS
> Printed by J. Baskerville in Birmingham, the same sized Paper and Letter with his Virgil. . . .

He was also planning the duodecimo *Horace* that was to appear in 1762. Shenstone makes the first of his many references to this book in a letter to Dodsley written on 11th February 1761.[4] "I have spoken to Mr L. upon the Subject of his Dedication; and he agrees with me that there can be no properer Person to procure the Leave we want than Mr D . . ."

The "Mr. L." of the letter was Livie, although there are variations in

---

[1] Williams CCLXXIII.
[2] See p. 91.
[3] Gaskell 15.
[4] Williams CCLXVIII.

the spelling of his name, who was a Latin scholar of some repute at that time living in Birmingham and acting as tutor to the children of Dr Roebuck. The "Mr. D." was Dalton, tutor to Lord Beauchamp. The "Dedication" being discussed was whether the *Horace* could be dedicated to Lord Bute, who must have agreed.[1]

Baskerville and his printers must have been busy for the whole of 1761. The *Juvenal* was published in May; he printed a three-volume octavo edition of the Works of Congreve[2] and a four-volume octavo edition of the Works of Addison[3] (both for J. & R. Tonson) in the same year (though Hanson suggests that the latter appears not to have been published until 1763[4]); he was High Bailiff of the town; he must have spent some time in Cambridge, or at least have been in correspondence with the University, negotiating to print a duodecimo prayerbook; he printed an ode to celebrate the royal marriage for Dodsley and others in September;[5] and he must also before the end of the year have begun to print the third edition of the octavo prayerbook as it was published in February 1762.[6]

One wonders how he managed to cope with Shenstone whose life in the second half of 1761 seems to have revolved around the forthcoming *Horace*, and indeed, to judge from the letters which have survived, Shenstone spent the rest of his life—he died on 11th February, 1763—writing to his many friends about the book.

On 11th June, 1761, he wrote to Thomas Percy saying he had received a specimen of the *Horace* "about twice as large as yᵉ small Elzivers"[7] and, having fretted slightly about the Elzevir omission of the semi-colon and the inconsistencies of other Elzevir punctuation, asks for advice. On 5th July he was wondering whether Baskerville should follow Bentley's edition of 1711.[8] On 17th September he wrote to Thomas Percy and criticises some of Baskerville's setting of the *Horace*, giving his opinion that the "scotch editor judges better, & his Edition *looks* yᵉ better for this Omission; tho I know B. lays no small stress on yᵉ beauty of his *Italick*

[1] see p. 77.   [2] Gaskell 16.
[3] Gaskell 17.   [4] Hanson: p. 140. and see p. 80.
[5] Gaskell 18.   [6] Gaskell 19.
[7] Williams CCLXXIV.   [8] Williams CCLXXV.

Type".[1] He presumably is referring to the Foulis books, as he does in a rather more interesting letter, written on 24th September to Mr. Mac-Gowan, late of Edinburgh:

> The Scotch press, of which you sent me so many agreeable specimens, has, I think, not a rival in world, unless it be that of my neighbour Baskerville. Here I find myself unable or unwilling to decide the preference. Amongst friends, however, I would whisper, that Baskerville's impressions are more striking to the eye, either on account of his ink, his paper, or his type: yet, at the same time, it may be much doubted whether the Scotch editions will not be deemed the best for use. Martial has expressed what *may* prove the case at the close of one of his epigrams:
> 'Laudunt illa, sed ista legunt'
> As to corrections, the Scotch seems to have hitherto the advantage; but if Baskerville find encouragement to print many Latin books, he purposes, I believe, to employ a Latin editor. There will shortly appear an Elzevir Horace from the press, revised by Mr. Levy, which you will probably like to see . . .[2]

In August he wrote to Thomas Percy saying that the book would be printed at the end of the month but not published before Christmas—he should have known better—and goes on:

> . . . It is really a beauty—and upon ye whole as good a *Text* as any we have *yet*—but excuse my vanity, who think I could have rendered it better: if they had suffered me to have the final determination of it. You know B. imagines y^t his *Letter* is *every thing*, on wch ye merit of a book depends . . .[3]

In January, 1762, writing again to Thomas Percy, he makes a rather strange remark about typographical design:

> I am not partial to a Full title-page, being a Passionate lover of Simplicity—You need not fear therefore, but I shall take care that

[1] Williams CCLXXVIII.
[3] Williams CCLXXXI.
[2] Williams CCLXXX.

Mine shall not offend you by its number of Parts—To say a Piece looks *busy* (crowded) is, wth Baskerville, one of the highest terms of Approbation—as it is with *Me*, a term of *Reproach*.[1]

This remark is so patently the reverse of what Baskerville practised that one wonders about Shenstone's hearing, or his veracity. But one forgives him on reading the letter he sent to the Rev. R. Graves on 20th November, 1762:

> There may be fifty or more preferable readings to what are received in this new Horace; yet he will find a better *text* there, *upon the whole,* than in any edition before extant. As to the *beauty* of *type* and *press-work*, it is too obvious to need vindication. The accuracy of the *latter* almost exceeds what was ever found in any other book. Then, as to the frontispiece, it is, I think, much superior to such as *ordinarily* occur; the subject animated, and well-chosen; and the execution very commendable . . .[2]

As was said above, Baskerville was doing other things as well as printing the Horace in 1761. The agreement with the University of Cambridge was made on 3rd July, and was to allow Baskerville to produce 4000 copies of a duodecimo Common Prayer. He was to pay the University £12. 10s. for each thousand, and had, as in 1758, to give security. He and Edward Robinson of London both gave security of £500.

The ode to celebrate the royal wedding had the formal title of *An Ode Upon the Fleet*,[3] and is a rather regrettable affair, poetically at least, about the fleet (including the Royal Yacht)[4] which went out to meet the Princess of Mecklenburg on her coming to this country to marry George III.

Shenstone did not think much of it. He wrote on 14th September, 1761 to Graves:

> . . . And last night was brought me, from Baskerville's press, on the same occasion, very pompously printed, the most despicable Grub-street I ever saw . . .[5]

[1] Williams CCLXXXVII.
[3] Gaskell 18.
[5] Williams CCLXXVII.

[2] Williams CCCI.
[4] Which is printed as YATCH on the title page.

This busy year closed with proposals being made to Baskerville to print an edition of Pope's works in quarto (mentioned in Nichols[1] as part of a letter written by Bishop Warburton). The scheme came to nothing, even though Shenstone mentions in a letter dated 16th May, 1762 that "Dr Warburton has, I hear also engaged Him to publish a Quarto— Edition of Mr Pope . . .", just after he had written that "Baskerville has of late been seized with a violent Inclination to publish Hudibras, his favourite Poem, in a pompous Quarto, with an entire new sett of Cutts . . ."[2] This latter scheme also came to nothing.

According to advertisements in *Aris*, Baskerville published "the Second Edition of An Octavo Common Prayer Book, long Lines, with Offices, on the largest Royal Paper . . ." on Monday, 15th February, 1762, and the same advertisement promised the duodecimo prayerbook[3] for April. Later in the year he published two books of psalms: *The Whole Book of Psalms*, Collected into English Metre, by Thomas Sternhold, John Hopkins and Others;[4] and *A New Version of the Psalms of David*, Fitted to the Tunes used in Churches, by N. Brady and N. Tate.[5] In a letter he wrote later in the year[6] Baskerville mentions that these books were intended to match the prayerbook, and he had to pay the Stationers' Company thirty pounds for permission to print one edition of the psalms in metre.

The duodecimo *Horace* appeared in May. *Aris* of 31st May carried an advertisement for it in these terms:

This Day is published, Price 5s. in Sheets
Elegantly printed by John Baskerville
Adorned with two new Designs engraved by Grignion
And inscribed by Permission to the Right Honourable the Earl of Bute
Quintus Horatius Flaccus
Accurante J. Livie, A.M.

although in *The London Chronicle* of June 15–17, 1762, it was also announced "This Day was published . . . etc." At the end of this latter advertisement was a list of the

[1] Nichols: *Lit. Anec.* V, p. 653 note.
[2] Williams CCXCIV.
[3] Gaskell 20.
[4] Gaskell 21.
[5] Gaskell 22.
[6] see p. 83.

Books Printed and Sold by John Baskerville in Birmingham.
Virgil in Royal Quarto, One Guinea in Sheets
Juvenal & Persius in Royal Quarto, Twelve Shillings in Sheets
Milton's Poetical Works, Two Volumes Royal Octavo, large Paper
  One Guinea in Sheets
A Prayer Book in long Lines, Royal Octavo, Eight Shillings and
  Sixpence in Sheets
Ditto———in Columns, Royal Octavo, Eight Shillings and Sixpence
  in Sheets
Ditto———in Duodecimo, Five Shillings in Sheets
Psalms to the Duodecimo Prayer Book, either Old or New Version,
  One Shilling and Sixpence in Sheets.

In view of the fussy attention the *Horace* had constantly received from Shenstone, and no doubt the careful proof-reading from Livie, its publication date must be considered remarkably early: the book had been mentioned for the first time only in February of the previous year. Gaskell even suggests[1] (as Shenstone said in his letter[2]) that the printing was almost finished by October 1761 but that trouble with the engravers held up the book's publication.

It is certainly true that in the advertisement of 15th February mentioned above, Baskerville said, "Also, a beautiful Edition of *Horace*, in Twelves, by John Livie, A.M. is now finished, and will be published as soon as the Frontispiece can be got ready." In two letters he wrote to John Livie in January and February, Shenstone is making plans for pressing on with the frontispiece and the decorations. In the first of these two letters, Shenstone writes as if "Mr Eaves" was looking after the affair for Baskerville. This, presumably, is Sarah's eldest surviving son whom Baskerville described later as his intended successor. The letters are not in Williams; they are in the collection of Baskerville material in the Birmingham Reference Library.

The *Horace* is an attractive and very charming little book. Harwood liked it very much:

[1] Gaskell: p. 42.
[2] see p. 75.

This is the most beautiful little book, both in regard to type and paper, I ever beheld. It is also the most correct of all Baskerville's Editions of the classics; for every sheet was carefully revised by Mr Livie, who was an elegant scholar . . .[1]

The only other books Baskerville produced during 1762 were printed for G. Steidel of Maddox Street, Hanover Square in London: Richard Gardiner's *Expedition to the West Indies* in quarto, the third edition (it was first published in 1759) and a French version of the same book.[2]

He did, however, produce a type-specimen[3] about this time. It is difficult to date the type-specimens of this period with any accuracy: none bears a date. One, without a border, was almost certainly printed in 1760; the other, with a number of variations in at least two editions, was produced in or around 1762. And it is probable that he began to print *Cinnabar and Musk* during the year,[4] and also the octavo Virgil.[5]

In the middle of 1762, Baskerville (possibly alarmed by the number of books he had still unsold and the obviously considerable amount of his fortune sunk in these and the Bible project) wrote to the Earl of Bute. The letter, preserved in the Bute family manuscripts at Mount Stuart was only recently recognised for what it is, and the first transcription appeared in a paper by James L. McKelvey in the *Transactions of the Cambridge Bibliographical Society* (Vol. V, pp. 138–41) published in 1971. The letter is mutilated, parts are missing—here indicated by (. . .)— but is endorsed "Birmingham June 1762. Mr. Baskerville requesting the humblest Employment as Printer in His Majesty's Service":

My Lord,

As My small Prayer book was (. . .) sizes only: I have taken the Liberty of sending a Specimen of all the Characters I have completed.

I hope Your Lordship will permit me without Offence, to lay before You the several difficulties I have laboured under in my Prosecution of the whole Scheme. It is now ten Years & half since I first began it at the Age of 46; It cost me above 1000 Pound before I

---

[1] Harwood: p. 226. [2] Gaskell 24, 25.
[3] Gaskell x. [4] see pp. 91–2.
[5] see p. 101.

returned a shilling. My first Attempt was a Virgil in 4to the Number 900, at a Guinea Subscription; the last 200 I was obliged to sell at fourteen shillings the Volume. I then applyed to the University of Cambridge (Oxford having farmed their Priviledge to the Patentee) & with Difficulty obtained their Licence to print an octavo Edition of a Common Prayer book in two Sizes of Characters, on the hard Condition of paying to the University twenty pound the thousand, & the expensive Inconvenience of setting up a compleat Printing House there; & the double Carriage of Paper to & from Cambridge, & afterwards to London &c; by the first Impression I was a loser, the Price being fixed too low to account for the extraordinary Expence.

I was very desirous of printing an English Classick, and pitched upon Milton; this I was sensible the Laws of my Country gave me a Right to, as an old Copy by a Statute 8th of Queen Ann 1710: but I was deterred from the Attempt, on an Information, that the Booksellers had entered into a Combination, and a Subscription to the amount of £3400 to ruin the Man who should invade their Property (as they called it) by printing an old Copy: this I have reason to believe was levelled at me, as it was not thought on 'till my printing appeared with some Reputation: But Mr Tonson who claims the Copy relieved me, by giving me Leave with the (. . .) print a large Edition of Milton's (. . .) me handsomely; I have since printed for him Addison's Works in four Vol. 4to royal not yet published as it stays for Prints; & Congreve's.

In July last I applyed again to the U^y of Cambridge for their Licence to print the above mentioned Prayer book in 12mo for the Use of Young People, which with the greatest Difficulty I obtained, on paying the U^y· £50 for the first Impression of 4000; and £10 the 1000 afterwards for seven Years. But finding the book not compleat without the Psalms in metre, I have obtained Permission of the Stationer's Company (who have engrossed both) to print the new version on paying them £12 the 1000 (which I am told is more than they sell their own Psalms for of that Size) and £4 the 1000 for the old Version.

The U^y has given me a Grant gratis (as it would not suit them to print such a one whether I did or not,) to print a folio Bible now in the

Press at Cambridge: which Grant, as soon as the Patentee was apprized of; he dispersed over the whole Kingdom proposals for printing a large folio Bible at little more than half the Price of mine; & refused a hundred Pound, which I offered him for his Leave to print mine at Birm^m nor should I ever have been able to have set about the Bible at all, but for the Assistance of my Patron Mr Tonson; who advances all the necessary Mony at 5 PCent on my own Bond. What Success that and my Prayer books may meet with God knows; I have nothing else to depend on.

Want of Business carried me to London latter end of March last; where I had hopes of printing Pope's Works in five Vol. 4to royal; but I could not succeed, tho' I offered to do it twenty Shillings the (1000) Sheet lower than I had been paid for Addison and Congreve; so that I have been forced to part with all my (. . .) on the Bible at Cambridge, having (. . .)

It is surely a particular hardship that I should not get Bread in my own Country (and it's too late to go abroad) after having acquired the Reputation of excelling in the most useful Art known to Mankind; while every Man who excels as a Player, Dancer, Fidler &c. not only lives in Ease & Affluence; but has it in His Power to save a Fortune.

Thus my Lord I have laid before You the naked Truth without Aggravation; and humbly hope your Lordship's Goodness will pardon the Presumption; for to whom could I apply but to Your Lordship, the Great Patron of Arts, under the Greatest and Best of Kings?

My humble Request to Your Lordship is, that the enclosed Specimen (if approved) may have the Honor of being handed to his Majesty. My Ambition would rise no higher than the humblest Employment in his Majesty's Service as Printer, were it Your Lordship's good pleasure to recommend me. The Patent I aim not at: I presume it was originally granted, and afterwards continued to preserve the Sacred Volumes from a mercenary Prostitution and Abuse, and Yet the present Sharers of it have gained an immense Fortune by the very Practice: The Bibles (especially for the Pocket) & Prayer books being worse printed, and on a worse Paper than any other the meanest Book that can be found in Britain. I should scorn to say this my Lord, were it not a notorious Truth known to, and lamented by the whole Kingdom.

Enclosed (. . .) Impressions of a Set of punches I have (. . .) Engraver to the Mint; designes for the Guineas. If approved I shall readily furnish all the Sizes of Letter for the whole Coinage; which I hope may add some Beauty; and make it more difficult to counterfeit the Currency. I have the honor of subscribing my self

Your Lordship's
Most dutiful & obed^t Servt
John Baskerville

PS. I printed 1000 of his Majesty's first most gracious Speech, so acceptable to the whole Kingdom, which I gave away, when I was informed the patentee claimed the sole right of printing them, as I did not choose to be in his Power.

McKelvey suggests that the reason why nothing came of this letter is that the Earl of Bute was too much engaged at the time with a major political crisis; or that he disapproved of Baskerville's views on religion.

Later in the year Baskerville was negotiating, according to a letter he wrote in 1773,[1] with the French Ambassador in London to sell the whole of his printing apparatus; and he also wrote to Horace Walpole:

Easy Hill Birmingham 2^d Novr 1762

S^r

As the Patron & Encourager of Arts, & particularly that of printing; I have taken the Liberty of sending you a Specimen of Mine; begun ten Years ago at the Age of forty seven; & prosecuted ever since with the utmost Care & Attention; on the strongest presumption that if I could fairly excel in this divine Art; it would make My Affairs easy, or at least give me Bread. But alas! in both I was mistaken. The Booksellers do not chuse to encourage me, tho I have offered them as low terms as I could possibly live by; nor dare I attempt an old Copy, till a Law suit relating to that Affair is determined.

The University of Cambridge have given me a Grant to print there 8vo & 12mo Common Prayer Books; but under such Shackles as greatly

[1] see pp. 130–1.

hurt me: I pay them for the former twenty, & for the latter twelve
Pound ten Shillings the thousand, & to the Stationers Company thirty
two Pound for their Permission to print one Edition of the Psalms in
Metre to the small Prayerbooks: add to this the great Expence of
double & treble Carriage, & the inconvenience of a Printing House
an hundred Miles off. All this Summer I have had nothing to print at
Home. My folio Bible is pretty far advanced at Cambridge, which will
cost me near £2000. all hired at 5 P. Cent. If this does not sell, I shall
be obliged to sacrifice a small Patrimony which brings me (...)[1] a
Year to this Business of Printing; which I am heartily tired of, &
repent I (...)[1] attempted. It is surely a particular hardship that I
should not get Bread in my own Country (and it is too late to go
abroad) after having acquired the Reputation of excelling in the Most
useful Art known to Mankind; while everyone who excels as a Player,
Fidler, Dancer, &c not only lives in Affluence, but has it in their power
to save a Fortune.

I have sent a few Specimens (same as the enclosed) to the Courts of
Russia and Denmark; and shall endeavor to do the same to most of
the Courts in Europe; in hopes of finding in some one of them a purchaser of the whole Scheme, on the Condition of my never attempting
another Type. I was saying this to a particular Friend, who reproached
me with not giving my own Country the Preference, as it would (he
was pleased to say) be a national Reproach to lose it: I told him,
nothing but the greatest Necessity would put me upon it: and even
then, I should resign it with the utmost reluctance. He observed, the
Parliament had given a handsome Premium for a quack Medicine; &
he doubted not, if my Affair was properly brought before the House
of Commons, but some Regard would be paid to it: I replyed, I durst
not presume to petition the House, unless encouraged by some of the
Members, who might do me the Honor to promote it, of which I saw
not the least hopes or probability.

Thus, S[r], I have taken the Liberty of laying before you my Affairs,
without the least Aggravation: and humbly hope your Patronage: To

---

[1] At this point the original letter is damaged. On a copy formerly in the possession
of Samuel Timmins "£74" and "ever" have been inserted.

whom can I apply for Protection but the Great, who alone have it in their Power to serve me?

I rely on your Candor as a Lover of the Arts; to excuse this Presumption in

Yʳ most obedient

and most humble Servant

John Baskerville

PS. The folding of the Specimens will be taken out by laying them a short time between damped Papers. NB. the Ink, Presses, Chases, Moulds for casting & all the apparatus for printing were made in my own Shops.

These are difficult letters to make any worthwhile comment on. The obvious question that cries out to be answered is why Baskerville wrote in such terms (some of them true, but others nearing untruth) and why, indeed, he was feeling so depressed about his printing venture. Trying to assess the reasons for a man's state of mind at a distance of two hundred years is a fatuous exercise: the letters must speak for themselves.

One is, however, tempted to wonder if domestic affairs were casting shadows on what, from his appearance and what is known of his normal behaviour, one would have thought of as a sanguine man. Richard Eaves, Sarah's husband who had left her in 1745, had recently returned to Birmingham, and this must have had repercussions on life at Easy Hill.

Whatever the reasons for Baskerville's state of mind in the second half of 1762, he could not have had a very enjoyable winter. John Eaves, Sarah's eldest surviving son, whom Baskerville regarded as his heir and successor, died in January 1763 (Bennett[1] records that he was buried at St. Martin's on 31st January) and William Shenstone died on 11th February. And it is certainly true that the only book Baskerville issued during the whole of 1763 was the folio Bible[2] and that was printed at Cambridge.

According to Hanson[3] the Bible was published on 4th July, 1763. It is

[1] Bennett I: p. 132. [2] Gaskell 26.
[3] Hanson: p. 139.

THE

CONTAINING THE

OLD TESTAMENT

AND

THE NEW:

Tranſlated out of the

AND

With the former TRANSLATIONS

Diligently Compared and Reviſed,

By His MAJESTY's Special Command.

❖✦❖

APPOINTED TO BE READ IN CHURCHES.

❖✦❖

CAMBRIDGE,

Printed by *JOHN BASKERVILLE,* Printer to the UNIVERSITY.
M DCC LXIII.

CUM PRIVILEGIO.

Title-page of the 1763 Bible *(reduced from 315 × 495 mm)*

THE

NEW TESTAMENT

OF

Our LORD and SAVIOUR

JESUS CHRIST,

Newly tranflated out of the

ORIGINAL GREEK,

AND

With the former TRANSLATIONS
Diligently Compared and Revifed,

By His MAJESTY's Special Command.

APPOINTED TO BE READ IN CHURCHES.

CAMBRIDGE,

Printed by *JOHN BASKERVILLE,* Printer to the UNIVERSITY.

M DCC LXIII.

CUM PRIVILEGIO.

Title-page of the New Testament from the 1763 Bible (*reduced from 315 × 495 mm*) certainly Baskerville's finest work: his 1769 Bible is a lesser book, in quality as well as size. It is equally certainly the finest book that had been produced in this country up to that time, and one of the three finest Bibles ever printed in England.

The adjective that inevitably comes to mind is "noble" and the volume warrants the word. It was conceived and executed on a grand scale, as the printer's masterpiece—to show that he had now learnt his craft and was able to practise it in a masterly fashion.

The title-page shows this beautifully in the scrupulously careful arrangement of roman and italic, upper and lower case; even more impressive is the skilful gradation of type sizes—there are nine on the page, as well as the two pieces of lettering on wood. These latter show a noticeable resemblance to the similar style of lettering on the advertisement slate cut about thirty years earlier.

As with the *Virgil* of 1757, the text-pages are equally well planned and executed. Looking at them, and comparing them with the suggested plans for the alternative styles of page lay-out shown in the Bible prospectus of 1760,[1] one can only be grateful to those of Baskerville's friends and clients who "objected to every Kind of Ornament round the Page". The final version is quite unadorned, relying for its effect on the careful arrangement of Great Primer set in two columns, each 28 pica ems wide and 62 lines deep. The running heads are set in Double Pica roman and italic, the notes at the head of each chapter in English italic, and the footnotes in Small Pica, roman and Italic. The result shows again that Baskerville must be placed in the very top rank of English book-designers.

[1] Gaskell: plates VI and VII.

5

✻❖✻❖✻❖✻❖✻❖✻❖✻❖✻❖✻❖✻❖✻❖✻❖✻❖✻❖✻

By the beginning of 1764, Baskerville was at least thinking of printing again. He must have had a letter from John Scott Hylton who lived at Lapal (the modern spelling) just outside the present Birmingham boundary. Hylton was a neighbour and close friend of Shenstone's and shared many of his interests and friends. Baskerville wrote to him:

> Birmingham 24 Jany 1764
> Sir,
>
> I should be glad to serve y^r Friend in printing his poem; my price is two Guineas the Sheet, without pressing, & two pound seven to be pressed as other Books which I have printed are. The difference between 1000 & 500 is to me inconsiderable as it is only Press Work. I have it not in my power to furnish the paper. I am
> > S^r
> > > Your most obed^t Servt
> > > John Baskerville

Hylton passed on the information to the Rev. Mr. Percy, who featured so largely in Shenstone's letters:

> Sir,
>
> I sent my servant last Tuesday to M^r: Baskerville, for his Answer to my letter concerning your enquires, and receiv'd the annexed Lines, which I at first thought to have transcribed, but afterwards concluded it would be more satisfactory to you to see them under his own hand; I ought to make an Apology for writing upon the same sheet, which

Sir,

Birmingham 24 Jany 1764

I should be glad to serve y^r Friend in printing his Poem; my Price is two Guineas the Sheet, without pressing, & two Pound seven, to be pressed as other Books which I have printed are. The difference between 1000 & 500 is to me inconsiderable as it is only Press Work. I have it not in my power to furnish the Paper. I am

Your most obe.^t Servt

John Baskerville

Baskerville's letter to John Scott Hylton

would not have been, but for the reasons given above, & to make the packet less.—Whether M^r: Baskerville's price is reasonable or not, you are the best judge, but I find by counting the Lines that it will cost somewhat about Twenty Guines to set the press, & how many copies he will work off for that price does not appear plain (to me), for his Letter indicates that 1000 or 500 may be nearly of a price to work off, as he cannot find the paper.

If I could serve you further in this Affair, I readily would, but as I scarcely go from home, (and never this wet weather) I can only serve you with my Pen, which you may freely command. Yet I dare say M^r: Baskerville would answer any Letter you might write to him upon This Subject.—I would only beg leave to mention, that if D^r: Grainger thinks proper to have his Poem printed by M^r: Baskerville, it would in my opinion be requisite to have a Friend upon the Spot, to inspect the press every Day, & who so proper as his Friend D^r. Roebuck, if he cannot attend it himself . . .

From D^r. Sir
Your most sincere Friend
John Scott Hylton

Lapall-House
   26 Janry. 1764.

Dr. James Grainger, who started this correspondence, was another of the Shenstone circle; he had just returned from the West Indies where he had written a poem in four books on the cultivation of sugar cane. He did not take up Baskerville's offer for the printing of the book. Dr. John Roebuck was a Scotsman living in Birmingham, a chemist who was making a good living by applying his knowledge to various branches of local industry. He it was who had employed Livie as a tutor to his children.

Nearly two years earlier, Shenstone had also given one of his friends some information about the cost of printing by Baskerville:

May 20, 1762

Dear Mr. Graves,
   . . . The expense of printing a sheet of those commendatory verses at

90

a common press is eighteen shillings: and at Baskerville's about three pound, ten shillings . . .[1]

If Shenstone's figures are right (particularly when one remembers the accusation made by Boden in 1769 about Baskerville's charges[2])—and he had had experience of having his own works printed—it is not difficult to see why Baskerville was short of work from publishers. Hanson[3] makes the point very elegantly: ". . . he resembled Oscar Wilde's acquaintance who dined *once* in every great house in London. Very few publishers asked Baskerville to print for them twice . . ." He points out as further evidence that Baskerville's Bible cost twice as much as comparable Bibles.

It has already been pointed out that Baskerville was a self-taught printer, who no doubt like anyone else in his position had to learn by making mistakes—and these are expensive. This, combined with his disregard of economic necessity (another amateur vice—or virtue, if one sees it that way) meant that he would produce only *de luxe* printing; and the market for this has always been small.

Baskerville printed three books dated 1764. One was a second edition of Dodsley's *Fables*[4] which had been foreseen by Shenstone in his letter in October 1761: "I fancy Dodsley thinks of causing Baskerville very soon to print a new Edition of his Fables: & to have the Designs I shewed you, engraved for it . . ."[5] Gaskell points out that the illustrations in the second edition are a mixture of the "closely similar but re-cut"[6] and others printed from the plates used in the 1761 edition. Although this book has the date 1764 on the title-page, it is very likely that it was not issued until 1766: certainly an advertisement in *Aris* would indicate this.[7]

The second 1764 book was *An Introduction to the Knowledge of Medals* by the late Rev. David Jennings, D.D.,[8] and Gaskell points out that the words of Greek and Hebrew which appear in the work seem to be set in Caslon type.

Yet in the third book printed this year (*The Virtues of Cinnabar and*

[1] Williams CCXCV.
[2] see p. 107.
[3] Hanson: p. 142.
[4] Gaskell 27.
[5] Williams CCLXXXI.
[6] Gaskell: p. 45.
[7] see p. 95.
[8] Gaskell 28.

Musk[1] by Joseph Dalby, Surgeon) Baskerville used some of his own Greek type. Gaskell draws attention to a variant title-page for this book which bears the date 1762, and Hanson says that this is explained by the death of Sir George Cobb in 1762.[2] The advertisement on the back of the title-page explains this:

> The following Sheets being wholly intended for the publick Good, it was thought but Common Justice to address them to Sir George Cobb, to whom we are indebted for the Knowledge of the Tonquin Medicine, against the Bite of a Mad Dog; but the Demise of that Gentleman happening while the Papers were in the Press, it is hoped that the Author may be excused the unnecessary Trouble and Expense of altering them.

Both variants were printed for the author.

It was in 1764 that Richard Eaves died and Baskerville married Sarah Eaves. Having settled his matrimonial affairs, he seems to have done something of the same kind for his financial affairs: in November 1764 he sold off his property in Wolverley, and thus, as Cave rather sadly writes,[3] gave up "an heritage of over 200 years . . . And so ends the Baskerville connection with Wolverley."

Robert Dodsley died on 23rd September, and Baskerville was in London late in October—whether as a result of this, one cannot tell. While he was in London he engaged in some negotiations for Matthew Boulton:

> White Horse, 24 Oct. 1764
>
> Dear Matt,
>
> To convince you that I am not unmindful of my Friends I last thursday waited on Mr Tonson, & proposed y^r affair. he desired a few Days Consideration: I this Day attended him again & had this Answer, that he would advance £3500 on a Security on one or two of your Estates of proper value at 4 p Cent Interest; As soon as this arrives, send the proper Writings to him to be examined, and as soon

---

[1] Gaskell 29.   [2] Hanson: p. 136.
[3] Cave: pp. 26–7.

as the Morgage is finished the Mony is ready. Pray give a line immediately to

Y^r affectionate

J. Baskerville

And, a week later:

White Horse 1 Novr 1764

Dear Matt,

In Consequence of my Credit & yours with Mr Jacob Tonson you may draw upon him for a Thousand pounds at seven days Sight, as soon as you please: He agrees that Mr Ingram shall make the Writings. The rest on Sunday. I set out to Morrow Morning.

yours affectionately

J. Baskerville

Both letters are preserved in the Birmingham Assay Office, and another preserved in the same collection shows even more how close Baskerville and Boulton were, both in business and friendship. The letter was addressed to "Mr. Boulton at Mr Motteux's a Merchant near the Mansion House, London":

Easy Hill 9 Decr 1765

Dear Matt,

I this Day made your Wife a Morning's Visit & found her in easy Health & good Humour. I found her quite reconciled to your Journey to Paris, & urged the Necessity of your Stay there to establish the trade that Oppenhiem used to have thro' his Hands. I told her that your sudden Departure left most of your London Business unfinished; that a Journey thither to meet you would agreeably accomplish the whole, that you would range 'till Dinner & attend her the Evening, that Dr Small would advise this & he observed that it would be as useful as a Journey to Bath, & the Consequence no doubt a son & heir, at which she laughed heartily, & said, then she would not go. I have the pleasure to inform you that Dr Small's affairs are become greatly more extended than when we left Bir. & some dangerous cases have offered, that greatly increase his Reputation, so that I took

93

the Liberty of saying what you had told me in Confidence in Relation to Russia; he replyed he had altered his Mind, as his practice (nearly) was as much as his Wish, but that he must go to London to thank Doctor Heberden for his kind Intention, which he could not so well do (or at least so respectfully) by Writing. I propos'd the D$^{r's}$ going as a favourable opportunity for Mrs Boulton, as he w$^{d.}$ attend in the double capacity of Guard and Physician; a line from you will I believe determine it. The D^r is informed that the Mine in the Highlands produces good black lead; but that the proprietor is a Minor; & that his Guardians will leave the working it, 'till he comes of Age. Pray acquaint me early what you do in the Lead Affair. After I had left my letter for you at Mr Motteux's I waited on Mr Tonson & told him the Affair intended; & asked him if he would lend you & I £1000 on our joint Bond; he answered, with all his Heart. I can faithfully assure you I have made great (speculative) Improvements in Pencil making after the sawing. If the Purchase does not take place, (as I hope it will) I sh^d be glad to purchase for my Self on the above presumption £30 or 40 Pounds worth of the very best; Pray try to see this Affair thro'

I am affectionately Yours

J. Baskerville

Nothing further seems to be recorded of the proposed venture into pencil-making, but although this particular business association appears to have come to nothing, the association between Baskerville and Boulton continued; and Boulton was of considerable help to Sarah after Baskerville's death.

Only two books were printed during 1765: Robert Barclay's *Apology* . . .[1] and *A Vocabulary or Pocket Dictionary*.[2] This latter was anonymous. The *Apology* . . . was the eighth edition in English, and was not printed for any specific bookseller. Bennett[3] suggests that it was printed to please the Birmingham Quakers and that Sampson Lloyd, a prominent local Quaker, founder of the bank which still bears his name, was responsible.

It would seem, if one can place reliance on the advertisements which

[1] Gaskell 30.　　　　　　　　　　　　　[2] Gaskell 31.
[3] Bennett: II, p. 9.

94

appeared for books in the newspapers of the time, that both these books were not published till the following year. In *Aris* of 7th April 1766 appeared the following:

> This Day are published
> Two new editions
> One in Octavo, printed by Richardson and Clark, Price bound 4s.
> The other in Quarto, printed by J. Baskerville; of Birmingham, Price bound 15s. of
> An Apology for the True Christian Divinity
> being an Explanation and Vindication of the Principles and Doctrines of the People called Quakers.
> By Robert Barclay . . .

and a fortnight later, 21st April, 1766:

> This Day is published
> A Second Edition of
> Dodsley's Fables
> Printed for J. Dodsley, in Pall Mall, by J. Baskerville
> And in a few Days will be published, a new Edition of
> Virgil in 12mo, in the same Letter and Size of
> Baskerville's Horace, and by the same Editor, John Livie, A.M.
> This day is also published, a Vocabulary, or Pocket Dictionary (to which is prefixed a Compendious Grammer) containing only such difficult Words as occur in genteel Company, and in those Authors which Ladies and Gentlemen may wish to form an Acquaintance with. It is presumed it may be of singular Use in Academies and Boarding Schools, as the young Scholars may learn the whole in a short Time by Way of Lesson.
> All printed by J. Baskerville and sold by . . .

It is in 1765 that Baskerville is supposed to have written to Benjamin Franklin offering his printing-house for sale to the French. William Hutton[1] appears to have been the first to say this. Both Chalmers and Nichols[2] repeat it in almost identical words: "In 1765, he applied to his

[1] *European Magazine*, Nov. 1785, p. 357.
[2] Nichols: *Lit. Anec.* III, p. 452.

friend the eminent Dr. Franklin, then at Paris, to sound the literati respecting the purchase of his types; but received for answer, 'That the
French, reduced by the war of 1756, were so far from being able to pur-
sue schemes of taste, that they were unable to repair their public buildings and suffered the scaffolding to rot before them.' "[1]

Baskerville was certainly in touch with Franklin (who had returned to
England for his second mission late in 1764) during this year as the latter
mentions him in a letter dated 22nd May 1765 to Matthew Boulton:
"Mr Baskerville informs me that you have lately had a considerable
addition to your fortune . . ."[2]

Yet Franklin does not appear to have been in Paris in 1765—he was
far too busy in London, and Kippis who was writing before Chalmers or
Nichols does not mention Baskerville's appeal. He does, however, tell
another story about Baskerville and the French, attributing it to John
Wilkes:

> Once, when Mr. Baskerville was in France, he was offered by the
> French King apartments in the Louvre for himself and all his appar-
> atus, and every kind of encouragement, if he would bring over and
> exercise his printing in Paris. This he refused to do because he would
> not deprive his own country of the credit of the art.[3]

It seems reasonable to assume that Hutton, Chalmers and Nichols
were antedating the 1767 letter from Baskerville to Franklin. In 1767
Franklin was in Paris from the end of August to the beginning of
October: Baskerville's letter was written at the beginning of September;
and the quotation from Franklin given above could very well be an
extract from an answer to this:

Easy Hill, Birm^m. 7 Sepr 1767

Dear Sir,

After having obtained the Reputation of excelling in the most useful
Art known to Mankind; of which I have your Testimony; Is it not to
the last Degree provoking, that I cannot even get bread by it? I must
starve, had I no other Dependence.

[1] Chalmers: IV, p. 107.   [2] Birmingham Assay Office.
[3] Kippis: III Corrigenda.

I have offered the London Book sellers to print for them within 5 per Cent. as low as their common Currency, but can not get from them a single Jobb.

I offered my whole Apparatus of Letter founding, printing &c. to the Court of France by the Duke de Nivernois when he was Ambassador here for £8000. which was politely refused as being too large a Sum.

Mr Godfroy, who may be heard of at Mr Sayde's Optitian to the King, lately told our good friend Mr Boulton, that France wished to be possessed of my printing &c. on moderate terms, in which I heartily join.

The Intention of this is therefore, to beg the Favor of you to propose and recommend this Affair, as Mr Godfroy may point out the Way. I want only to set on Foot a Treaty; if they will not come to my Terms, I may possibly come to theirs.

Suppose we reduce the price to £6000. Lewis the 14th would have given three times that Sum, or Czar Peter. Let the Reason of my parting with it be, the Death of my son and intended Successor, and having acquired a moderate Fortune, I wish to consult my Ease in the Afternoon of my Life, as I am now turned of 60. I am Dear Sir, with the greatest Esteem your most obedient humble Servant,

John Baskerville

It is as impossible to say why, after a gap of five years, Baskerville again was trying to sell his printing business as it is to say what caused him to write to Lord Bute and Horace Walpole in 1762, or to try in that same year to negotiate a sale with the French ambassador.

The whole of what Wm. P. Barlow, Jr. calls "the between Bibles period"[1] is full of difficulties and insoluble problems. The usual explanation advanced is that Baskerville became disenchanted with printing and publishing when he found that his Bible did not sell, that he had sunk far too much money into the printing venture, and that he gradually handed over the press to Robert Martin and concentrated his energies on his japanning business—only to return to the press in indignation when

[1] In correspondence and conversation.

97

Boden and Adams announced that their Bible title-page would be superior to his.[1]

Barlow has in his collection a manuscript diary of a two-week trip made in 1765. The two travellers were "Thos. Hull and Jn. Mulford"; their journey took them, on Thursday 11th July, to Birmingham; and they had this, among other things, to say about the town:

> . . . & here the ingenious Mr. Baskervil who made those curious Types for Printing so much resembling Copper Plate engraving as not to be distinguish'd from it. His ingenuity not only led him to make the Types but even the paper and Printing presses The Books he printed are a Church Folio Bible a Common Prayer, Milton's paradise lost & regained in large Octavo and some others. He has now quitted that branch of business for Waiter making being Iron japane'd, pierced & some beautifully painted. . . .

The idiosyncratic ideas Messrs. Hull and Mulford had about the use of capital letters and punctuation make it difficult to realise at first sight that the last line of the passage is a reference to making trays (Baskerville described himself in 1770 as "Japanner of Tea Tables, Waiters, Trays etc."[2]) from sheet iron which was japanned and decorated in various ways.

It is certainly true that of the books printed in the five years 1764–68 almost all show problems of publication date, being issued at least the year after the date shown on the title-page, or being begun well before they were issued. The best example is the octavo *Virgil* which seems to have been four years in the making.[3] And in the two years 1767–68, Baskerville produced no books at all.

Another observable fact is that of the eight books printed with Baskerville's name on the title-page, only three were not printed for the authors or for booksellers, and of these three, one has a variant title-page bearing the phrase "Printed . . . for T. Field . . . and J. Payne . . ."[4]

There is almost no information to be gathered from other sources about what Baskerville was doing during these five years. We know that

[1] see p. 105.   [2] see p. 10.
[3] see p. 101.   [4] Gaskell: pp. 45–51.

he lost apprentices and advertised for replacements in 1766 and 1767.[1] This seems to have little significance: the Birmingham paper carried advertisements about absconding apprentices in almost every issue. In December 1765 he and his wife donated, respectively, ten and five guineas to the newly launched appeal for a proposed General Hospital in Birmingham. In February 1767 he lent Matthew Boulton the sum of £1470.[2] He can hardly have been living in penury to have done either of these things. In March 1768 he advertised for a young milking cow which had strayed from Easy Hill—a fascinating glimpse of life in eighteenth-century Birmingham, but hardly helpful to our knowledge of Baskerville's work at the time.

Even the books do not help. There is no perceptible falling-off of the standard of printing in the books bearing Baskerville's name; and even though the books Robert Martin printed under his own name are, on the whole, badly printed (by Baskerville standards) at least one of them would not have disgraced the master. This is *The Chase, A Poem* . . . by William Somerville, published in 1767.[3] The inking is not as good as the best of Baskerville's books, but the design could have been, and possibly was, done by Baskerville himself—certainly no other book printed by Martin has anything of this quality. The others are rather mean-looking and cramped in their design; and when Martin began to print for himself after Baskerville's death, the books he produced then were typical of eighteenth-century provincial printing at its worst—even the Baskerville type could not save them.

The most disturbing problem (to the present writer, at least) of this period is Martin's takeover of the press. He certainly produced books under his own name during the years 1767–68, and he used Baskerville's type and, presumably, his presses. He also, according to Boden during the controversy over the Bibles in 1769, seems to have used the presses for printing other people's work.[4] Yet the only information we have about this is the advertisement quoted by Straus and Dent, and by Bennett. They both give identical announcements, taken from *Aris*.

---

[1] see p. 10.
[2] Document in Assay Office.
[3] see p. 102.
[4] see p. 108.

Robert Martin has agreed with Mr. Baskerville for the use of his whole printing apparatus, with whom he has wrought as a journeyman for ten years past. He therefore offers his services to print at Birmingham for Gentlemen or Booksellers, on the most moderate terms, who may depend on all possible care and elegance in the execution. Samples, if necessary, may be seen on sending a line to John Baskerville or Robert Martin.

Straus and Dent date this advertisement as June 8, 1768;[1] Bennett dates it June 16, 1768.[2] On neither of those dates was a copy of *Aris's Birmingham Gazette* published; and, in fact, the present writer has found it impossible to discover the advertisement at all.

Whether this is another of the apocryphal stories which surround Baskerville, it is impossible to decide; for one cannot be certain that there is *no* such advertisement—anyone who has read copy after copy of an ill-printed eighteenth-century newspaper will know how impossible it is to be absolutely certain that one has not missed a vital news-item or an announcement. What is certain is that Martin had, in September 1767, already announced proposals for printing his *Shakespeare* with "Baskerville's types".[3]

It is also necessary to correct a remark made by Bennett when he suggests[4] that in 1766 Thomas Warren was acting as local agent for the sale of remaindered Baskerville prayerbooks. He refers to an advertisement by Warren in *Aris* of 12th May, 1766:

This Day is published
At the easy Price of Two-Pence (to be continued Weekly, till the whole is finished) elegantly printed with a large Letter on fine Demy Paper,
Number 1 of
The Book of Common Prayer, and Administration of the Sacraments. . . .

The advertisement specifically says that the book is printed by Warren,

[1] S. & D.: p. 55.
[3] see p. 102.
[2] Bennett: II, p. 13.
[4] Bennett: II, p. 24–5.

who also offers to print, letter-press and copper-plate, for customers; and a glance at a copy of Warren's prayerbook shows it to be printed in a very ordinary type; the book is certainly not a remaindered Baskerville prayerbook.

Three books were printed in 1766 and after that year Baskerville's name did not appear on a book again until the beginning of 1769. The books were: *The Works of Virgil, Englished* by Robert Andrews; *Odes* by Robert Andrews; an octavo edition of Virgil's *Bucolica, Georgica et Aeneis*.[1]

The Latin Virgil had been foreseen as long before as 1762 when Shenstone writing to Percy on 10th August said: "Baskerville has begun to print a Virgil of ye size of the Spectator, which I think a better yn that of his Horace."[2] Whether Baskerville managed to publish the book at the time he said in his advertisement of 21st April quoted above[3] we cannot say (in that advertisement he described the book as 12mo; it is in fact Post octavo) but he was sending copies to Livie (whom he still persists in calling "Livy") in December, and this seems a long time to have kept his editor waiting if indeed the book was published in April or May:

> Easy Hill, 3 Decr. 1766

Dear Livy,

I shall send you by tomorrow night's waggon to the care of Robinson three Virgils, & would have added as many Horaces, but my wife's zealous impatience would not suffer me to stay for the Binding. If you want more to oblige friends or will point out anything else that will do Mr Livy a pleasure, it will be a particular one to

His obedt & obliged servant

J. Baskerville

The Virgil translation by Robert Andrews was published in May and his *Odes* in November, according to Gaskell, although Hanson gives advertisements in London papers saying they were published in April and September.[4] Both books were printed for the author. On 28th September 1767 Martin announced in *Aris* that:

[1] Gaskell 32, 33, 34.   [2] Williams CCXCVIII.
[3] see p. 95.   [4] Hanson: p. 204.

This Day is published, Price 3s. in blue paper,
The Chase, to which is added, Hobbinol; Or, the Games,
a Burlesque Poem in Blank Verse.
The Author, William Somerville Esq;
This Work is printed with a large Type in Octavo,
on a fine Royal Paper, and finished in an elegant
Manner by Robert Martin, and sold by him in
Birmingham, and by A. Donaldson, Bookseller, in the
Strand, London; and by all Country Booksellers.
And Nov. 5 will be published the First Volume of
The Works of William Shakespear,
And continue a Volume every Month, till the Whole is
finished: each Volume to contain four Plays, sewed in
Blue Paper; they will be elegantly printed with
Baskerville's Types, on fine Demy Paper, with Notes
from Pope, Warburton, Theobald, &c. in 12mo.
The Price to Subscribers will be two Shillings the Volume. . . .

He repeated the advertisement the following month, and on November 2nd he advertised the following:

Proposals for Printing by Subscription
Excise, a Poem, with Poems upon several Occasions
   By R.S. in Birmingham
         Shall I the snarling Critics fear?
         Be gone ye testy Tribe!
         'Tis Freedom's Right to claim an Ear;
         Subscribe, my Friends, subscribe. R.S.
Conditions. This Work will be printed in Mr. Baskerville's Types, and to be contain'd in one Volume, stitch'd, at the Price of two Shillings and Six-pence, to be paid upon the Delivery of the Book. . . .

But the proposals appear to have come to nothing in spite of the delightful example of an early advertising jingle. Martin also produced *Words of One Syllable* during the year.

Martin began issuing his *Shakespeare* on November 5th and, to judge by his advertisements, he continued it until it was complete. He had, however, to publish an advertisement in June 1768, apologising for falling behind in his programme. Also, during 1768 he printed *The Lady's Preceptor* for Edward Johnson at 12 Ave-Mary-lane in London and *Elogy on Prince Henry* (and a French version of the same work) for Peter Elmslet in the Strand.

In the issue of *Aris* dated 30th May, 1768 appeared the following, in the column of news from Birmingham:

> Thursday last Mr Baldwin, Bookseller in London, purchased of Mr John Baskerville, of this Town, the remaining Copies of his very elegant Folio Bible; and we are informed that the Number amounted to near 500.

although Baskerville himself said in 1770[1] that he sold 556, at thirty-six shillings each, having printed 1250.

On 13th June, 1768, *Aris* carried an advertisement announcing the publication, in parts, and beginning on 4th July, of a "Most Elegant Family Bible". There was no mention of who was printing and publishing it. The following week the proposals were printed in full: that it should appear in weekly parts, price twopence half-penny; that it should be completed in 150 parts; that it should be Folio Demy; that it should be printed "with an entirely new letter, closely copied from Mr Baskerville's, and cut on purpose". Subscriptions were to be taken in by a number of Midland booksellers, and they were asked to send the account of numbers already subscribed for to "Mr O. Adams, Printer in Worcester-street, Birmingham".

Orion Adams was a printer who had been born in Manchester where his father was a printer and proprietor of *The Chester Courant*. He had wandered from town to town and had finally settled in Birmingham. He seems to have gone into partnership with Nicholas Boden for this Bible venture, although Boden's name does not appear in the advertisements until early the following year.

The "New letter" of the advertisement was obviously Fry's Baskerville[2] which had recently become available from Bristol. The text was

[1] see p. 117.   [2] see p. 166.

certainly set in this letter (of which the printers seem not to have had a large supply as in the third part issued they had to use an inverted "p" for the "d", of which, presumably, they had run out). The chapter-headings and other display work are carried out in what are almost certainly Caslon faces although, as the work progressed, Fry's Baskerville was bought in a great variety of sizes. Some of the type may even be authentic Baskerville, but the work is so badly printed that it is difficult to be absolutely sure about this. Some pages are decorated with the "lozenge and star" ornament of which Baskerville was so fond.

The weekly parts were produced on time according to the almost weekly advertisements, and by 1st August the first part was having to be reprinted, as were parts 3, 4, 5 and 6 by October. The same advertisement which announced this offered a set of copperplate engravings for the Bible, and on 5th December 1768 it was announced that the subscription list for the engravings was full, that a third edition of part 1 of the Bible had been published, and that the faulty part 6 would be replaced.

During December there was an altercation in *Aris* between T. Smith of Wolverhampton, who had announced the publication in parts of *The Christian's Best Treasure,* and the still-anonymous printers of the Bible who, according to Smith, were distributing handbills announcing the imminent publication of *An Illustration of the Book of Common Prayer* which he thought an attempt to injure the sale of his work.

The printers of the Bible were shortly to be the victims of a similar attempt and to be involved in a more serious and lengthier controversy. On 26th December, 1768 there was an advertisement in *Aris* announcing part XXVI of the Bible, in the usual terms, but after that appeared the heading "A Caution to the Public" and under that an announcement that "Boden and Adams, Printers in Birmingham, and Proprietors of the most Cheap and Elegant Bible that was ever offered to the Public" (this is the first time that the printers of the Bible revealed their responsibility for it) had discovered that one of their agents in the Lichfield, Burton, Derby and Nottingham area had been suborned by a rival organisation and was offering subscribers a different work. The rest of the announcement is taken up with extravagantly phrased praise of their Bible and its success, and a solemn undertaking to finish the work.

The advertisement also included a new offer: "That with last Number shall be given gratis, a General Title, much more beautifully and methodically displayed than that in Mr. Baskerville's, and an elegant Copper-plate Frontispiece."

The reason for all this is revealed by an advertisement which appeared lower down in the same column of the newspaper:

> Proposals for publishing by Subscription, A Complete Family Bible, in Folio, containing the Sacred Texts of the Old and New Testaments at Large, and the Apocrypha, with Notes and Annotations . . . by Robert Martin, Printer, who for this Purpose has engaged the elegant Apparatus of Mr. Baskerville's Printing House, and Foundery, the Beauty of which in the Letter, Ink and Printing, has been allowed by all Europe to excel whatever of the Kind has gone before it. Conditions. As the Editor is determined to spare no Trouble or Expence to make the Work complete it will be printed on a superfine Demy Writing Paper, and intire new Letter, which has never been inked, the Text in size English, and the Notes Brevier, once a Fortnight till March, and then weekly. That it will be published in Numbers (the first to appear the 2nd of January next) at Fourpence Half-penny each. That the whole will be comprized, as nearly as can be calculated in 79 Numbers, which will bring the Expence of the Volume to about thirty-one or thirty-two Shillings.
>
> Gentlemen and Ladies who choose the Volume complete rather than the Trouble of taking them in Numbers, are desired to send their Names and Places of Abode to Robert Martin, at his House in Birmingham, and their Favours shall be duly regarded and acknowledged.

What happened at Easy Hill around Christmas 1768 will never be known, but one suspects it was that "Title, much more beautifully and methodically displayed than that of Mr. Baskerville's" which really did the damage. On 2nd January, 1769, the following appeared in *Aris*:

This Day is Published

Price Two-pence Halfpenny, Number 1 of A Complete Family Bible, in Folio . . .

By John Baskerville.

Conditions As the Editor is determined to spare no Trouble or Expense to make the Work complete, it will be printed on a superfine Demy Writing Paper, and entire new Letter, which has never been inked.

II That the Whole will (as nearly as can be calculated) be comprised in 130 Numbers, which is less by 20 than that published by Boden and Adams; so that if any one who prefers this to theirs, and even sinks all their Numbers as waste paper, will only pay fifteen-pence in the whole Volume more than if they continued to take theirs.

III That one Number will be published every Monday till the Volume is finished.

N.B. Gentlemen and Ladies who choose the Volume complete, without the Trouble of taking them in Numbers, are desired to send their Names and Places of Abode to the Editor, who will deliver to them the Volume press'd and fit for Binding, but without Gloss, at the same Price the Numbers will amount to.

Boden and Adams having taken an indecent liberty with the Editor's Name, in saying of their Letter, *closely copied from Baskerville's,* and in promising a *Title much more beautifully and methodically display'd than Baskerville's* before it was set up. This has induced him to the present Publication, that their Copy may be compared with his original Letter. The Title will speak for itself. I. B. begs Leave to inform those who are Strangers to it, that in the Year 1758 he had the Honour to be appointed Printer to the University of Cambridge, by their whole Body in Convocation, under their great Seal, in order to print several Editions of the Common Prayer in three Sizes, which he executed with the highest Approbation of the University, and for which he paid a large Acknowledgment. These several Sizes he purposes to publish in weekly Numbers: the first on 9th January, with Proposals to be then exhibited.

The Intention of this is to guard the Public against the bare-faced Effrontery of Two Publishers in the Paper, of Illustrations of the

Common Prayer, as it arrains the Reformation, and calls in Question the Abilities of the whole Body of the Clergy in Convocation; whose immortal Honour it is to be the Compilers of the most pathetical Form of Prayer that the Wit of Man ever invented.

The following week he repeated the advertisement, with an example of the size of the text type of the Bible inserted (perhaps rather foolishly, as it was set in what looks like a Caslon letter) and he points out how much cheaper his Bible will be than his rivals'.

In an adjacent column appears a rejoinder from Boden and Adams:

Mr Baskerville in an Advertisement he published in last Week's Paper, seems to be very angry with the Proprietors of this Bible, because forsooth, they have declared to the Publick, "that their Letter was closely copied from his"! See how Men may be mistaken; we designed to compliment Mr Baskerville, and I believe all who have themselves the Trouble to read our Advertisement thought so too; but I cannot help thinking Mr Baskerville in the Case is like the Wolf in the Fable, who wanted an Occasion to fall out with a Lamb, and not having sufficient Ground for a Quarrel, accuses the poor Lamb with muddying the Brook while he was drinking, though the Lamb stood far down the Stream; the Moral of this Fable is, that when an envious ill-natured Man is determined to quarrel, he will always find a Pretence: But I believe we need not take any Pains to convince the World that Mr Baskerville has other Reasons, not only for this Publication, but for rummaging up all his old Prayer Books;—enough of that;—I have now his Advertisement before me. In his First Condition, he says, his Work shall be printed "on a superfine Demy Writing Paper, and a Letter which has never been ink'd"; now any Persons who will give themselves the Trouble to examine, will find what he calls a Writing-Paper. to be a very thin poor Rag; and if he was to ink his Letter properly, the print would be seen quite thro' it . . . In regard to Mr Baskerville's Printing the World seems to have adopted a wrong Notion; that he has done some Things well, is very certain, but then they should consider that he has had at least three Times the Price for his work any other Printer ever had before him;

but now we have tied him down; and, notwithstanding all his pompous Puffs, we can assure the Public that our Work, for many reasons we can give, is at least equal, if not superior to any Thing he can produce at the Price; that he cannot print better is very certain, because part of this very work was printed at Baskerville's Printing-Office, under the Inspection of his oldest Man, Martin, who he says has now engaged his whole Printing-Office.

I believe we need not take any more Pains to explain to the World Mr Baskerville's real Motive, and have not the Least Doubt but our good Friends will support us under his ill-natured Opposition.

Boden and Adams

Any person who has been induced, thro' Mr Baskerville's Puff, to subscribe to his poor Production, may have it exchanged gratis for our elegant Work, by applying to the Printers in Worcester-street.

It may be thought that this was hitting below the belt, but the following week (16th January, 1769) a much more personal and scurrilous note enters the controversy (although one must admire the phrasing and vocabulary employed):

Mr. Boden presents his Compliments to Mr Baskerville, and informs him, that if he, (Mr Baskerville) had begun a Work of this Kind, without attempting to depreciate ours (as Things are Circumstanced) the World could only have blamed him for an ill-natured ill-timed Opposer; but as it is very evident he aimed at nothing less than the Destruction of a Man who never offended him, he has brought upon himself an almost general Odium: However, I would advise Mr Baskerville to use every honest Art in his Publication, but in future to let Invective alone, for if he perseveres, he may be assured that I can brace a DRUM that has long lain dormant, and will beat such a Travally, that he will heartily repent he ever opposed us; Mr Baskerville began the Attack, and if God grants me health, I'll fight the Battle through . . .

And under that advertisement appears another:

Proposals for printing by Subscription

A Treatise on Atheism by Nicholas Boden of Birmingham
Assisted by several learned Gentlemen
In this Treatise will be introduced the Whole Life, Character and
Opinions, of a Commentator on the Holy Scriptures.
Subscriptions are taken in by the Author, at his House in Worcester-
street; no money will be required till the Book is delivered, nor any
more Printed than are subscribed for.—The Author returns his sincere
Thanks to the Gentlemen who favoured him with the Anecdotes
relating to Walton, the Conjurer, and for those contained in the
BONNY ROACH: all other authentic Anecdotes will be thankfully
received, and faithfully inserted.

In the same issue Baskerville writes:

> *. . . He that has but Impudence,*
>   *To all things has a fair Pretence:*
>   *And put among his Wants but Shame,*
>   *To all the World he may lay Claim.*   Hudibras

Would any Man, who has a Grain of Reputation to lose, have made
so open an Attack upon it as N. Boden has done upon his own? by
asserting the most scandalous falsehoods, and such as cannot go un-
detected two Hours; for Instance, that my Paper was a poor thin Rag,
and if I was to Ink my Paper properly it would be seen quite through;
a most impudent Assertion, which the Title and every Page of the
Book will contradict. The Paper cost Fifteen Shillings and Six-pence
per Ream in London and is as good as can be had in England for
Printing: My Printing is, and always has been strictly in Register, one
line falling on the Back of the other, which preserves the Colour and
Beauty of the Whole, and is best seen when held up to the Light, by
those who are not Criticks in Printing: Boden and Co. have paid no
Regard to this, either through Neglect or Incapacity, probably the
latter. Add to the above the following Instance of their Disingenuity,
which proves their Design is only to deceive the Public, to wit; that
my first Number does not take in so much as theirs by two Chapters . . .
It would be descending below myself to take any further Notice of
these Gentlemen (who are lately started such from the Obscurity of

Journeyman Printers) or of their Publication, least the bare noticing of their feeble Attempt should make them fancy themselves of as much Importance as the Frog in the Fable did, who would needs be as great as the Ox; they may swell with Pride, Envy and Self-Conceit till they burst.

Therefore their impudent Falsehoods, Ignorance and Scurrility, want of Decency and good Manners, will be no more an Object at all worthy the Notice of

John Baskerville

Indeed, he was true to his word, for the following week the advertisement for his Bible had no further contribution to the controversy.

Boden, however, had to reply to the previous week's attack. He first promised that his Bible would be completed in fewer numbers than Baskerville's. He borrowed Baskerville's idea of showing the size of text type in the advertisement, and more sensibly than Baskerville, provided the printers of the newspaper with a line of the actual type (and he also scored another point by choosing to set "The fool hath said in his heart there is no God"). He then went on:

... Mr Baskerville says he had the Honour to be appointed Printer to the University of Cambridge, for which he paid a large Acknowledgment, and that his Printing has been admired all over Europe: the first of these Assertions, in my poor Capacity, is a Contradiction of Terms; and the last, in my firm Belief, an absolute Falsehood: For it is not many Months since he sent his Man, Martin, to London, for Orders, with his best Piece of Printing, which he hawked about to the Booksellers, by Way of Pattern Card, promising that he would print at London prices: It availed him nothing! They did not like it! They would not employ him!—I call upon Mr Baskerville to dispute the Truth of this? His Letter too has been offered to every Kingdom in Europe and rejected by all; and if he keeps it a few Years longer in his Hands, he will be beyond all Comparison excelled by Mr Isaac Moore, in Queen-street, Moorfields, London ...

Mr. Boden begs leave to inform his Friends, that some Anecdotes he has received this Week to be inserted in his Treatise on Atheism, are so full of Lewdness and Debauchery, that he is apprehensive they will be incompatible with the more serious part of his Treatise, on which Account he is advised to decline the Atheistical Subject, and only write the History of the Commentator and his Family.—The Work will be embellished with several copper-plates; the Story of one in Particular will be taken from a very interesting Scene the Hero was concerned in, with Walton the Conjurer. It will now be published as a Novel, with this Title "The History of John Bull and his Family" wherein

I will a round unvarnished Tale deliver
Nothing extenuate, nor set down ought in Malice . . .

The readers of the newspaper must by now have been approaching satiety (though the proprietors of the paper must have been grateful for the increased advertising revenue), for in the following week's issue (30th January 1769) there was the following item in the column of Birmingham news:

The following Lines are humbly addressed to Mr B—— and Co.
and Mr B——
Let Sacred Penmen mind their Text,
Not pers'nal Comments *make,*
Lest your Subscribers *are perplext,*
And Scripture Rules *forsake*

A SUBSCRIBER

And in this issue there is only a little sniping at each other by the printers (Baskerville saying that subscribers would be well advised to trust their money to a "Man of Known Property"; Boden talking about his engravings).

The advertisement from Baskerville in the issue of the newspaper dated 6th February announces that he had "near two Thousand Subscribers to his Bible in Numbers, and near one Hundred for whole Volumes". Boden, however, published a letter from Grignion saying he received a promise of a thousand guineas to engrave the plates for Boden's Bible, and underneath:

This Day is also Published
Proposals for Printing by Subscription
The History of John Bull and his Family, a Novel, founded on Facts
By Nicholas Boden, of Birmingham. . . .
N.B. This Work will make one Volume in Octavo, price three
Shillings: but for the Convenience of those who do not chuse to lay
out so much Money at one Time, it will also be published in 12
Three-penny Numbers.
The Anecdotes concerning the Jew, and those of A. D. W——th's
Family are come safe to Hand.
This Work will be entered at the Hall, therefore I caution Mr.
Baskerville against re-printing it . . .

This proposal, like the proposal for Boden's *Treatise on Atheism*, came
to nothing and are obviously just methods of telling Baskerville that
Boden knew of scandals and skeletons in the Baskerville family cupboard.
Nevertheless, however scandalous they were, one would dearly like to
know, possibly above all others, the details of the affair of Walton, the
conjurer.

The advertising for the rival Bibles went on for the next four months,
with little or no controversy. At the beginning of March, Boden announced that the free title-page would be delivered to subscribers the
following week and it would be set in "letters, cut by Mr Isaac Moore,
late of this Town, which, for Size and Beauty, are superior to any ever
cast by Mr Caslon, or any other Letter Founder in Europe".

The Boden title-page is indeed a handsome piece of setting in Fry's
Baskerville, an obvious copy of the 1763 Baskerville title-page, even to
using a very similar wood-engraved "Holy Bible" in black-letter. If the
type, and indeed the whole page, were not such an obvious copy, one's
admiration for it would be high.

On 10th April, the Boden advertisement announced that Adams was
leaving the partnership; the Baskerville advertisement mentioned that
he still had copies for sale of Milton's *Poetical Works*, Two Volumes,
Royal Octavo; Somerville's *Chase* . . .; Dodsley's *Fables*; and *A Vocabulary*. On 22nd May, Boden advertised:

This Day is Published
Proposals for Printing by Subscription
The Atheist, a Poem
By N. Elliot, of St. Ebb's Lane, Oxford (Author of The Vestry) . . .

and proposals for an edition of Shakespeare's *Plays*. Baskerville included the edition of Shakespeare printed by Martin the previous year in his advertisement a fortnight later.

The Atheist was not a mere debating-point as Boden's other proposals had been: it was published the following year. Most of it, text and display, is set in Fry's Baskerville with an occasional letter from another fount. It is a rather tedious poem of over 650 lines, full of self-righteous platitudes about the wicked. There is one obvious reference to Baskerville in lines 646–9:

> *And when the measure of thy days is full,*
> *And thou are gather'd to the mighty dull,*
> *Curst be the hand which violates thy will,*
> *Or robs thee of thy favourite vault, a Mill**

* A real Fact, too well known to need an explanation

The reference to the "vault" and the footnote is made clear by Baskerville's will which he must have been talking about, even though he did not make it formally until 1773.[1] Strangely enough, not a single Birmingham name appears in the list of subscribers printed in Boden's book.

[1] see pp. 122–6.

6

All this controversy with Boden, or possibly the success of his Bible in parts, obviously gave Baskerville a new lease of life—at least as far as his printing was concerned. In 1769 he printed at least two books other than the Bible in parts, and a third book may have been printed by him.

The two on which his name appeared are: *A Sermon Preached at Bromsgrove*, by Thomas Tyndal; and *The Beauties of Nature . . .* by W. Jackson.[1]

The *Sermon* was preached at the funeral of Mr John Spilsbury who died on 27th January, 1769. It is unlikely that the book was published before April as it is not included in the list of books for sale in the advertisement mentioned above.[2]

The Beauties of Nature . . . is a more substantial volume and was published by 4th September when it was advertised in *Aris*. Proposals for printing it by subscription had been advertised in that newspaper, the previous year in July and August, making no mention of Baskerville or Martin. The advertisement of the book's publication merely says: "Printed by J. Baskerville, for the Author, and sold by him and Mr. Morgan, Bookseller, in Lichfield."

The third book was *The Life and Political Writings of John Wilkes, Esq. . . .* This is doubtful, though both Gaskell[3] and Straus and Dent[4] list it as Baskerville's work. Its title-page merely bears the words "Birmingham: Printed for J. Sketchley and Co. MDCCLXIX". It is certainly set in authentic Baskerville (mainly Small Pica and English) but some of the display letters are suspect. It is difficult to imagine Baskerville designing

[1] Gaskell 36, 37.
[2] see p. 112.
[3] Gaskell 38.
[4] S. & D. 84.

114

or allowing the title-page to be set: it is messy and cluttered. His lozenge and star ornament is used, but on page 520 there is a group of six-pointed stars which Baskerville never used and which were not shown on any of his type-specimens. The inking throughout the book is lamentable by Baskerville standards. If he did print it, it is certainly the poorest work he produced.

The book may, of course, have been printed by Robert Martin—or by one of the other Birmingham printers who seem at about this time to have acquired some genuine Baskerville type. This latter possibility is fairly remote as most of them seem to have had very little type. The various books referred to by Hill or Straus and Dent as being in Basker-ville's type usually prove to have only a line or two set in genuine Baskerville. And even then it is impossible to be absolutely certain as the standard of their printing makes definite recognition of type a difficult matter.

In the period between 1769 and Baskerville's death in 1775 the follow-ing printers seem to have had small amounts of genuine Baskerville type and ornaments—particularly the "lozenge and star"—which they usually used for a line or two of display work on title-pages or elsewhere:

Christopher Earl	(although his *Collection of all the Airs. . . .* 1769, quoted by Straus and Dent[1] has only a few genuine Baskerville letters on the title-page)
Myles Swinney	(Hill mentions advertisements set in Baskerville type in newspapers published in 1771 by Swinney[2])
Thomas Chapman	(but the text of his *Judas Macchabeus*, 1774 is set in Baskerville's Pica roman with an occasional letter, usually upper-case, from another fount)
Luckman & Lesson	(several pamphlets printed by them in 1771 had an occasional display line set in Baskerville's types)
Samuel Aris	(at least one pamphlet, *A Letter to Mr James Turner* [1771] had some display lines set in Baskerville's types, although the text was set in Fry's Basker-ville)

[1] S. & D.: p. 89.   [2] Hill: plate facing p. 40; p. 85.

Also during 1769 was printed the fifth of Baskerville's pieces of jobbing printing to have been discovered. This was *Verses in the Character of a Corsican* . . . by James Boswell,[1] who records in his diary that he set out from London on 5th September 1769 to attend the Shakespeare Jubilee at Stratford-upon-Avon. He arrived there on Wednesday, 6th September and then writes:

> Thursday 7 September. . . . This was the night of the ball in mask, when I was to appear as a Corsican chief. I had begun some verses for the Jubilee in that character but could not finish them. I was quite impatient. I went home and forced myself to exertion, and at last finished what I intended. I then ran to Garrick, read them to him, and found him much pleased . . .
> There was a fellow called Fulk Weale here, who advertised "printing at an hour's notice". I suppose taking it for granted that Stratford would produce a general poetic inspiration which would exert itself every hour. To him I went. But Mr Angelo's fireworks turned his head and made him idle. I then went to the bookseller and printer of the place, Mr Keating. He had a lad from Baskerville's at Birmingham, of Scots extraction, his name Shank. I found him a clever, active fellow, and set him to work directly. He brought me a proof to the masquerade ball about two in the morning. But could not get any verses thrown off in time for me to give them about in my Corsican dress . . .[2]

Gaskell mentions a facsimile of the verses produced at Stratford (not set in Baskerville's type) and suggests that "Shank" took a copy back to Birmingham where it was re-set and printed by Baskerville. Only one copy is known, in Yale University Library. Gaskell reproduces it[3] and it has all the hall-marks of Baskerville's setting: the widely spaced capitals; the use of italic capitals; the very wide range of type-sizes used; and the use of the very rare swash capital "M" in the word "James". This all seems conclusively to dispose of any idea that it may have been printed by any other printer.

[1] Gaskell xiii.   [2] *Boswell in Search of a Wife*, pp. 292–300.
[3] Gaskell: Plate IX.

The only other recorded information about Baskerville in 1769 is that discovered by Langford.[1] During the year an Act was passed for "Laying Open and Widening certain Ways and Passages within the Town of Birmingham . . ." Among the Commissioners appointed to see the Act carried out was John Baskerville.

The next year, 1770, saw Baskerville return to printing the classics—although he continued with other projects—and this programme was to be continued almost to the end of his life.

At the beginning of the year, however, he had some trouble about an injunction that was brought against him by Baldwin, the London bookseller. On 1st January 1770, the following advertisement appeared in *Aris*:

> In the year 1758, J. Baskerville had the honour to be made Printer to the University of Cambridge; in Consequence of which he printed in 1761, an edition (1250 in Number) of the grandest and most elegant Folio Bible, that ever appeared since the invention of the Art of Printing, whose published Price was Four Guineas.
>
> In the year 1768, Mr R. Baldwin, Bookseller, of London, purchased all the remaining copies of the said Bible (in Number 556) at Thirty-Six shillings the Volume; but declining to pay the balance, J. Baskerville brought an Action against him for 100*l*. 16s. In order to stop Proceedings at Common Law for a short Time, R. Baldwin filed a Bill in Chancery; and by his Affidavit, that the Bible J. Baskerville was now publishing in Numbers, was IN ALL RESPECTS the same as that sold to him, (except the Addition of a few Notes) obtained an injunction from the Court of Chancery prohibiting the said J. Baskerville from publishing any more Numbers of his Bible, till this Affair is determined, which will be on or before the 12th Instant; so that every one who has subscribed to his Bible may depend on being served regularly after that Time.
>
> J. Baskerville

A fortnight later the case had still not been heard, and the following week (22nd January, 1770) he quoted a letter from his Attorney in

[1] Langford: I, p. 190.

London saying the case was to be heard on "Tuesday next". The following week (29th January) Baskerville advertised:

> Mr Baskerville begs Leave to acquaint the Subscribers to his Complete Family Bible, that the Injunction against his Publication is now taken off; and that they shall be regularly served with the Numbers till the Volume is completed.

Bennett[1] suggests that the taking out of this injunction was inspired by Boden as a final act in the controversy of the previous year. Baskerville himself suggests it was to prevent Baldwin having to pay his debts. One wonders if the fact that Baldwin was about to publish a Bible in parts (he advertised it in *Aris* on 26th February) had anything to do with it.

The first classic to be printed in the programme was a quarto *Horace*.[2] It was the only one of the series of classics he produced during this period to have plates, although Gaskell records that, while the frontispiece appears in all the copies he has seen, the other four plates appeared in only half. Straus and Dent[3] call it "the rarest of the quarto classics"; Horne[4] calls it "the rarest of all Baskerville's editions"; and it certainly did not appear in the list of the book stock Sarah was trying to sell in 1775.

On 17th September 1770 an advertisement appeared in *Aris*:

> This Day is Published, Price Six-pence,
> An Essay towards publishing A SYNOPSIS OF THE GENERAL PRACTICE OF PHYSIC.
> Translated from the Latin of Joseph Lieutaud, Chief Physician to the Royal Family of France. By. T. Tomlinson. Printed by J. Baskerville . . .

When Gaskell wrote his *Bibliography*, no copy of this was known to exist. Hanson,[5] however, describes a set of Proposals for publishing the work, and Gaskell lists it in his second edition.[6]

[1] Bennett: II, p. 24. [2] Gaskell 39.
[3] S. & D.: p. 60. [4] Horne: p. xc (Appendix).
[5] Hanson: p. 138. [6] Gaskell 40.

The only other book with the date 1770 is *Grace Triumphant* . . . By Philanthropos [John Fellows] . . . Birmingham . . . MDCCLXX.[1] It is an octavo volume printed for the author, in Baskerville's type, but does not bear his name.

However, during the year Baskerville also issued his first proposals for *Orlando Furioso*.[2] There was, in fact, some doubt whether there ever was a proposal dated 1770 as the only copy seen and described by Gaskell is dated 1772. Hanson, however, mentions a copy dated 1770 now at the Oxford University Press.[3] Some of the volumes of the work itself bear the date 1771 and Baskerville would certainly have printed proposals before he printed the book.

He must have been printing *Orlando* for most of 1771: the only book he issued during the year was *The Political Songster* by J. Free.[4] This was an octavo, printed for the author; Baskerville's name appears on the title and it was sold by two Birmingham booksellers. This is not surprising as "Free" was John Freeth, a local man who had some reputation as a poet. He published a number of books of political and satirical verse. A Book called *The Political Songster*: containing Twenty New Songs . . . Printed for the Author . . . was advertised in *Aris* in 1766 (3rd November) but no details of author or printer were given; and no copy seems to have survived.

In October 1771, Baldwin inserted a surprising advertisement in *Aris*:

This Day was published
Baskerville's Royal Folio Bible for Churches, Chapels and Libraries
R. Baldwin, at No. 47 Pater-Noster-Row, London having purchased the remaining copies of Mr Baskerville's Folio Bible, which for Beauty of Paper and Type, exceeds any Thing of the kind ever issued in this or any other Kingdom, and were sold by him at Four Guineas in Sheets, proposes selling the remaining Books at only Three Guineas each till further Notice . . .

These must be the last of the Bibles he had bought over three years before, and the payment for which Baskerville said was the cause of the

---

[1] Gaskell 41.   [2] Gaskell xiv.
[3] Hanson: p. 137.   [4] Gaskell 42.

litigation at the beginning of 1770. There seems no reason why Baldwin should have decided to advertise them in Birmingham at this time, unless it was to anticipate the completion of the Demy Bible in parts, which had been begun in 1769.

The dealings over the commission to print *Orlando* may have given Baskerville ideas, for in 1771 he made an approach to Voltaire with what was almost certainly a suggestion that he should print an edition of some of Voltaire's writing. Baskerville's admiration for Voltaire was well known, and he probably decided to combine his own interests with what, pretty certainly, would have been a safe commercial project.

Baskerville's letter to Voltaire no longer exists but Voltaire's reply does:

> au chateau de Ferney, par Genève
> 2e 7bre 1771
>
> Sr,
> I thank you earnestly for the honour you do me. I send you oane exemplary by way of Holland.
> I am yr most obdt st.
> Voltaire
> Gentleman of the M:C: King's Chamber

As Besterman says in his commentary on the letter,[1] "the facts are clear: Baskerville had obviously written to inform Voltaire that he intended to print an English edition of his works, and to ask for an approved text; the present note is Voltaire's reply . . ."

Baskerville must have received "the exemplary" and returned it, for there is another letter from Voltaire:[2]

> 16e 9bre 1771
> à Ferney, par Genève
>
> Sr,
> The old scribbler to whom you have been so kind as to send yr magnificent editions of Virgil, and Milton, thanks you heartily.

[1] Besterman: Letter 16304.
[2] Besterman: Letter 16404.

He will send you as soon as possible his poor sheets Duly corrected. They stand in great need of it.

Yr most h: obdt st

V . . .

The project was still in being in December, for there is a reference to it in a letter written by Joseph-Marie Durey de Morson who was at Ferney, acting as copyist to Voltaire, on 3rd December 1771. Translated, the letter says:[1]

> A group of rich Englishmen, living near London, wish to produce a fine edition of all the Nestorian works.
> Nestor, loving fame, is putting his hand to it, he is making corrections, cuts and additions to his own works which my pen copies every day.
> Although I have not been expressly told it is confidential, I beg you, Gentlemen and dear Friends, not to divulge it . . .

But nothing came of the project and no one knows why.

The year 1772 is the year of the quarto classics. Baskerville printed and published three of these in this one year, as well as issuing two of them in duodecimo. There seems to be something of a pattern in this printing of Latin classics: he issued the *Virgil* in quarto in 1757, and the *Juvenal* quarto in 1761, the *Horace* in 1762; three quartos in 1772 and one in 1773. Each of these (except the *Virgil*, re-issued as an octavo in 1766, the *Juvenal* which was not re-issued, and the *Horace* of which the duodecimo ante-dated the quarto) were issued also as duodecimos. And, sadly, most were still in stock in substantial numbers in 1775;[2] the only ones sold out were the 1757 *Virgil* and the two editions of *Horace*. There were even 250 copies of the *Juvenal* left; and it had been published 14 years before, in 1761. One wonders why Baskerville did it, especially as the country was, in 1772, going through what we would now call a recession.[3]

[1] Besterman: Letter 16444.
[2] see p. 139.
[3] Bennett: II, p. 30.

The 1772 quartos were: Lucretius, *De Rerum Natura*; Catullus, Tibullus and Propertius, *Opera*; Terence, *Comoediae*. The duodecimos were: Catullus etc. and Terence.[1]

The 1772 proposal for *Orlando* was printed in French and was for a four-volume edition, in octavo, of *Orlando Furioso*, by Ariosto, to be published by the firm of Molini Brothers, who were probably the leading European booksellers of the time. They commissioned the letterpress from Baskerville, which the prospectus says had already been completed. Gaskell[2] suggests that it was probably completed in 1770 (although 1771 does seem more likely) and the plates (a frontispiece and 46 others) not completed till late in 1773. Hanson puts the date even later.[3] One wonders who wrote the text of the proposal and suspects that perhaps the none-too-modest hand of Baskerville himself can be seen in the (translated) passage:

> The Molini Brothers have undertaken to issue an edition of him [Ariosto] which will satisfy the desires of the Public, and match the reputation of this great Man. They have used the presses of the famous *Baskerville*, whose Masterpieces of Printing the whole world knows and admires. This edition will not fall short of those he has already issued . . .

In January 1773 Baskerville made his will. It is a long document, mainly concerned, obviously, with the bequests he wanted to make to various of his relations, but it must be seen in full as it is certainly the document most revealing of his character that is extant. The most important characteristic which emerges from it is integrity. He was a kindly man—this is clearly revealed as it was in his life (particularly in his treatment of Sarah); but he was stubborn, and he did not forget slights easily. Nor did he possess any false sentimentality: his reference to the possible future re-marriage of Sarah disposes of that, even though at her age the possibility was remote. He was realistic and just: see his reference to Rebecca and Thomas Westley. The passage which refers to his burial place and the reasons for it are obviously the sincerely-held

---

[1] Gaskell 43–7. [2] Gaskell: p. 64.
[3] Hanson: p. 205.

beliefs of a man who not only had an independent mind, but was capable of coming to a carefully thought-out set of beliefs and of then continuing to hold them in the face of what must have been considerable unpopularity. One can only admire him:

Memorandum that I, John Baskerville of Birmingham on this sixth day of January 1773 do make this my last Will and Testament as follows: First I give bequeath and devise unto my executors hereafter named the sum of two thousand pounds in trust to discharge a settlement made before marriage to my wife Sarah. I also give to my executors the lease of my house and land held under the late Jonathan Ruston in trust for the sole use and benefit of the said Sarah my wife during the term of her natural life and after her decease to the several uses mentioned below and my further will is that the above sum of two thousand pounds shall be raised and paid to my wife out of my book debts stock in trade household furniture plate and china. N.B. the use of my furniture plate and china I have already given by deed to my wife for the term of her natural life but this will make it entirely her own. I appoint and desire my executors to take an Inventory and Appraisement of all my effects whatsoever within six weeks after my decease. I also give to my executors hereinafter named the sum of one hundred pounds in trust to the sole use and benefit of my nephew John Townsend to whom also I give my gold watch as a keepsake. I further give to my executors in like trust the sum of one hundred pounds for the sole use and benefit of my niece Rebecca the wife of Thomas Westley as an acknowledgment of relationship. I have heretofore given by Will to each of my last named relations a more considerable sum but as I have observed with pleasure that Providence has blessed their endeavours with success in acquiring a greater fortune than they will ever expend the income of and as they have no child or chick to inherit what they leave behind them I have stayed my hand and have hereby reserved a power to assist any branch of my family that may stand in need of it. I have the greatest respect and esteem for each of the above persons. I also give to my executors in like trust the sum of one hundred and fifty pounds for the use of my nephew Richard Townsend Butcher. I further give to my executors the sum of three hundred pounds to be disposed of as follows to Joseph Thomas and Jacob sons of Thomas Marston by his wife Sarah my niece one hundred pounds each as they severally attain the age of one and twenty years but should any of them die before they come of age then such hundred pounds shall be divided share and share alike among the survivors. I also give to Isaac the son of Thomas Marston ten pounds for pocket money and the reason is his being patroniz'd by his worthy uncle Thos. Westley who if he behaves well will put him in a way to acquire an easy fortune. But I must not forget my little favourite. I therefore give to my executors in trust the sum of five hundred pounds for the sole use and benefit of Sarah the daughter of Ferdinand and Sarah de Mierre my wife's daughter to be paid her when she attains the age of twenty-one years but should she happen to die before that age my pleasure is that my wife shall have the disposal of the said five hundred pounds at her own pleasure signified in her last Will. I also give to my executors the further sum of fourteen hundred pounds in trust to the following uses viz. to Rebecca Westley John Townsend Richard Townsend and to the four sons of Thomas Marston by his wife Sarah my niece two hundred pounds each to become due and payable (only) on the day of my wife's future marriage which if she chooses I wish her happy equal to her merit but if she continues a widow the last legacies are entirely void. I further give to my executors in trust all my goods and chattels household furniture plate legacies and debts not disposed of as above to the following uses, 1st for the payment of the legacies and debts to the creditors of all the residue remaining except the sale of my lease as below to the sole use and benefit of my wife Sarah. I further give to my executors in trust the reversion of the lease of my house and land held under my good friend the late Jonathan Ruston together with fixtures in the house particularly the fire place including the grate fender etc. together with three leaden figures, all my plantations of trees and shrubs of every kind including my grotto and whatever contributes to beautify the place, that the whole shall be sold by publick auction after being properly advertised in some of the London and neighbouring country papers, the money arising from such sale I give to the following uses: viz, £500 to the Committee for the time being of the Protestant Dissenting Charity School at Birmingham in trust towards erecting a commodious building for the said Charity, £700 more arising from the said sale I give and bequeath as follows, £400 to be shared equally among the sons of Thos. Marston by his late wife Sarah, to John and Richard Townsend my nephews £100 each, to Rebecca Westley my niece £100, and my will is that this and the above mentioned sum of £100 shall be entirely at her disposal and not subject to the control or intermeddling of her husband. Her receipt alone shall be a sufficient discharge to my executors. £500 more arising from the said sale I give to the three sons of the late Jonathan Ruston, even and equal shares to Jo, Dan and Josiah. What further sum of money may arise from the sale of the above lease I give to the sole disposal of my wife Sarah by her last Will—as I doubt not the children of my late worthy friend will endeavour to traduce my memory as they have already done my character. In leaving my lease on too easy terms I therefore think proper to declare that at the time I took the aforesaid lease I paid the full value of it and have laid out little less than £6000 on the premises, but as the increase of the town has enhanced its value, I have made on it as above, which I always proposed to the sons of my most valued friend, which would have been much more considerable if they had refrained from injuriously abusing me. I had even given the reversion of my lease to Martha Ryland upon the death of my wife's eldest son and my intended successor, but her unprovoked and petulant malice and spleen and abusive treatment of me convinced me of the rancour of her heart and I determined as above.

My further will and pleasure is and I hereby declare that the device of goods and chattels above is upon this express condition: That my wife in concert with my executors do cause my body to be buried in a conical building in my own premises, heretofore used as a mill, which I have lately raised higher and painted, and in a vault which I have prepared for it. This doubtless to many may appear a whim, perhaps it is so, but is a whim for many years resolved upon, as I have a hearty

125

contempt for all superstition, the farce of a consecrated ground, the Irish barbarism of sure and certain hopes etc. I also consider revelation as it is called, exclusive of the scraps of morality casually intermixt with it, to be the most impudent abuse of common sense, which ever was invented to befool mankind. I expect some shrewd remark will be made on this my declaration by the ignorant and bigoted, who cannot distinguish between religion and superstition, and are taught to believe that morality (by which I understand all the duties which a man owes to God and his fellow-creatures) is not sufficient to entitle him to Divine favours without professing to believe as they call it certain absurd doctrines and mysteries about which they have no more conception than a horse. This morality alone I profess to have been my religion and the rule of my actions to which I appeal how far my profession and practice have been consistent. Lastly I do hereby appoint my worthy friends Mr. Edward Palmer and Josiah Ruston my wife's brother joint executors to this my Will in the most perfect confidence as I know the integrity of their hearts that they will jointly and cordially execute this my most important trust committed to them with integrity and candour. To each of which I leave six guineas to buy a ring which I hope they will consider as a keepsake. In witness whereof I have to this my last Will put my hand and seal the day and year above written.

John Baskerville

The Epitaph
Stranger—
Beneath this Cone in unconsecrated ground
A friend to the liberties of mankind directed his body to be inhum'd.
May the example contribute to emancipate thy mind
From the idle fears of superstition
And the wicked arts of Priesthood.

(The passage from "the farce of unconsecrated ground . . ." to "which ever was invented to befool mankind" was omitted by Nichols[1] with the comment: "What follows is by far too indecent for repetition.")

[1] Nichols: *Lit. Anec.* III, p. 452 note.

The period 1772–4 must have been one of the busiest periods of Baskerville's life—certainly in his printing activities. In 1773 he issued a three-volume edition of Shaftesbury's *Characteristicks* and two editions of classics, as well as probably printing one other book.

The two editions of the classics were the duodecimo *Lucretius*[1] to match the quarto of the previous year, and a quarto *Sallust and Florus*.[2] They are in all ways similar to the classics already printed in this period.

The three-volume octavo Shaftesbury[3] was the fifth edition of a work first published in 1710. Bennett suggests[4] that there "can be little doubt that Baskerville's edition . . . was printed by the master of Easy Hill as an expression of his own religious opinions founded on the Deistic philosophy of Shaftesbury". It seems more likely, and more in keeping with Baskerville's character, that he printed it purely for commercial reasons; but there were still copies left in stock at his death. The work is decorated with a portrait of the author and a number of vignettes.

The doubtful book printed in 1773 is a duodecimo *Hymns on Believers Baptism*[5] by John Fellows, the author of *Grace Triumphant* (1770). The title-page merely says: "Birmingham. Printed for the Author and sold by G. Keeth, *Grace-Church* Street and J. Dermer, *Shad Thames* London." It is printed in Baskerville type but does not bear his name.

In view of all the printing and publishing activity of the 1772–74 period, one passage in a letter which Baskerville received in September 1773 from Benjamin Franklin is very significant; and the whole letter is interesting:

London, 21 Sept. 1773

Dear Sir,

I duly received your favor, and some time after the packet containing the specimen and your valuable present of Shaftesbury, excellently printed, for which I hold my self greatly obliged to you. The specimen I shall distribute by the first ship among the printers of America, and I hope to your advantage. I suppose no orders will come unaccompanied by bills or money, and I would not advise you to give credit, especially as I do not think it will be necessary.

[1] Gaskell 50. [2] Gaskell 51. [3] Gaskell 49.
[4] Bennett: II, pp. 32–3. [5] Gaskell 52.

The sheet of chinese paper, from its size, is a great curiosity. I see the marks of the mould in it. One side is smooth, that, I imagine, is the side that was applied to the smooth side of the kiln on which it was dried. The little ridges on the other side I take to be marks of a brush passed over it to press it against that face on places where it might be kept off by air between, which would otherwise prevent it receiving the smoothness. But we will talk further of this when I have the pleasure of seeing you.

You speak of enlarging your foundry. Here are all the matrices of Rumford's and James's founderies to be sold. There seems to be among them some tolerable Hebrews and Greeks, and some good blacks. I suppose you know them. Shall I buy them for you? I thank you for your kind invitation. Perhaps I may embrace it for a few days.

My best respects to good Mrs Baskerville, and believe me ever, with great esteem, etc

B. Franklin[1]

The "specimen" is presumably a type-specimen, probably that originally issued in 1762 and as Gaskell suggests kept in print until 1775 when Sarah issued the last but one of the type-specimens. The temptation to comment on Franklin's opinion of the credit-worthiness of his compatriots must be resisted.

It is the third paragraph which is so significant. Baskerville was in the middle of what is the most productive period of his career as a printer and was considering enlarging his foundry: his recovery from the depressions and doubts of the 1760s seems to have been complete.

It is, of course, impossible to make any realistic comments on the reasons, but one wonders if the enquiries he had received during the year from France had had any effect on his state of mind.

Early in June 1773 Baskerville received a letter from Philippe Denis Pierres, a French printer. Pierres had, three years earlier, been appointed "Premier Imprimeur Ordinaire du Roi" and was engaged in compiling information about printing and presses. He wrote a number of articles on typography and at least one book, on a new press he invented, 1786,

---

[1] Jay: p. 30.

and one on the art of printing[1] in a series, *Collection des Arts de l'Académie des Sciences.*

Pierres' letter and Baskerville's reply do not appear to have survived, but at the beginning of December, Baskerville received his letter back from Paris marked "not known". He sent a second letter:

Birmingham 2ᵈ Decʳ 1773

Sir,

Your Favour of 2ᵈ June came duly, which I reply'd in a Week after, but this day I was surpriz'd at its being return'd, charg'd 2/3. & on the back was written that the Person directed to could not be found in Sᵗ· James Street Paris.

My Letter was to the following Purport. You are Pleased to make me a Compliment in supposing I have a superior Knowledge in the Art of Printing, it is indeed a Compliment; for if I have excel'd, it is in the Execution . . . [see p. 28 for this passage].

You are pleas'd to ask for a Description, Drawing &c of my presses; I have answer'd that above. I referred you in my last to Palmer's History of Printing in 4º: but since my writing a much more valuable Book has fallen into my Hands (to wit) The History & Art of Printing in 8ᵛᵒ by P. Luckombe, printed for J. Johnson, St Paul's Church Yard, London, in which you have a Print of every part of the Press.

As to yʳ last Request of giving you two Lines of each Size of my Characters to insert in your intended Work, I reply'd that I had but one Objection to it, and that was, that it was not in your power to do them Justice when us'd among other Types, but lest you should think this too assuming, I enclos'd to you a Specimen, and have in this sent another.

I am, Sir, with due Respect,
Your most obedient Servᵗ.
John Baskerville
over

As I am come to a Resolution to sell Types occasionally, if you will

[1] B. & W.: II, p. 202.

give me the Length of your Line, & the Matter you intend setting up, I will send to y^r. Order to any Person in London, who will receive and pay for them, the two Lines of each Size in my Specimen, which you desire & a Fount of any Size in my Specimen.

The letter was addressed:

> to Mr Pierres an eminent Printer at
> Paris
> To the Care of Mr Molini a Printer
> there

but he crossed out the second "Printer" and substituted "Bookseller".

The Palmer's *History of Printing* referred to was published in 1729, in parts, and in 1732 and 1733.[1] Philip Luckombe's book had been first published, anonymously, in 1770, and was re-issued in 1771; it contained some practical instructions—"the United opinions of the most experienced of the trade".[2]

Pierres may have mentioned that he was intending to use the information he hoped to obtain from Baskerville in his book for the Academy of Sciences, for Baskerville wrote at the same time to the President of the Academy (which had some responsibility for the Royal Printing House in France). It is interesting that about eighteen months later, Harwood, writing the Preface, dated 25th April, 1775, to the first edition of his book on editions of the classics,[3] refers to the "Royal Typography in the Louvre . . . of Lewis XIV" and suggests that His Majesty should institute a similar printing-house in this country with "the purchase of the late Mr Baskerville's types or *matrices* . . ."

This is the letter to the President of the Royal Academy of Sciences:

Honoured Sir.

I some years ago made a Proposal of selling to the Court of France my whole apparatus of Letter-founding & printing; (Viz) Puncheons Matrices Moulds; Presses Chaces Cases &c &c and several Tons of Types & Type Metal; for the whole I asked eight thousand Pound,

---

[1] B. & W.: II, pp. 109–11.   [2] B. & W.: I, p. 447.
[3] Harwood: pp. x–xii.

& for which I had the Honour of treating with the late Duke of Nivernois; & after with their Excellencys Messrs Guerchy & de Eon, while Residents here; the Result was, that the Court of France did not accept my Proposal.

If the enclos'd Specimen has Merit enough to attract y^r Notice, and it is your Pleasure to recommend it to his most Christian Majesty, I shall be proud of the Honour of furnishing the Royal Printing House at Paris with any, or all the Sizes contained in the Specimen. I have two Sizes larger that could not handsomely be brought into it.

You will at a Glance observe, that my Letters are not (one of them) copyed from any other; but are wrought from my own Ideas only: I was brought up to no kind of Business; but had early in Life a great Fondness for Print Characters.

I have never sold any Types, nor do I intend to sell any to London Printers, as my Labours have always been treated with more Honour abroad than in my native Country.

I have given a Copy of my Reply to Mr Pierre's Letter, that if your honourable Society should have any Commands, they may safely reach the Hands of

Your most obed^t hble Servt

John Baskerville

Baskerville's treating with the Duke of Nivernais, d'Eon and Guerchy must have been at about the same time as he wrote to Walpole in 1762, for the Duke came to London as French Ambassador in September 1762 and returned to France the following year; d'Eon was the Duke's secretary and was in control of the embassy until late in 1763 when Guerchy replaced the Duke.

In 1774 Baskerville completed his series of the classics by producing the duodecimo *Sallust and Florus*[1] to match the quarto edition of the previous year, and in the same style as the other duodecimo classics.

Three other books were produced during the year. One, *Six Views of Believers Baptism* by John Fellows,[2] duodecimo, second edition (although some copies are known with "third edition" on the title-page) was

---

[1] Gaskell 55.   [2] Gaskell 54.

printed in Birmingham, for the author, but does not bear Baskerville's name.

The second, *The Art of Angling and Compleat Fly-Fishing* . . . The Second Edition, By Charles Bowlker of Ludlow is "Printed by John Baskerville for the Author".[1] It is a duodecimo and has no date on the title, though the Preface is dated 4th May, 1774.

The third is the last book Baskerville printed: *The Anatomy of the Human Gravid Uterus* by William Hunter.[2] It is among the finest of his books, a magnificent volume of text and plates, the text printed one page at a time and bound unfolded. It is larger in format even than the Folio Bible, although it contains only 21 pages of letterpress and 34 copperplates. The text is printed in parallel columns of Latin in roman type, English in italic. The title-page is also printed in both languages: the Latin upper half set in roman, the English lower half set in italic. In this half is a very rare swash capital V and the less rare swash capitals A and M. The two halves of the page are separated by a line of the rococo ornament.[3] It is a handsomely designed page, an ingenious solution to the problem of two-language setting.

A paragraph in the Preface[4] gives a rather unusual reason for having a book printed by Baskerville:

The additional expense of Mr. Baskerville's art was not incurred for the sake of elegance alone; but principally for the advantage of his paper and ink, which render a leaf of his Press-Work an excellent preservative of the plates between which it is placed.

The book was priced at 6 guineas and was published early in December.

Baskerville died in January, 1775. All the biographers, with the exception of Hutton, who merely says he "died without issue in 1775, at the age of 69",[5] say that the date was 8th January.

Yet *Aris* did not carry the news of his death till the issue dated 23rd January, when it said:

Died. On Monday last, at Easy Hill in this Town, Mr John Basker-

[1] Gaskell 53.
[2] Gaskell 56.
[3] Ornament No. 2 in S. & D., Plate XIV.
[4] p. 4.
[5] *European Magazine*, November 1785, p. 357.

ville; whose Memory will be perpetuated, by the Beauty and Elegance of his Printing, which he carried to a very great Perfection.

The 23rd January 1775 was a Monday, which means that—if one believes the paper to be accurate in its reporting—that Baskerville actually died on 16th January. As he was buried in his own grounds at Easy Hill, there is no other record to act as a check on this date.

The *St James's Chronicle* announced his death in a column headed "Saturday, January 21" in the words: ". . . A few days ago, at Birmingham, Mr Baskerville, a Printer."

One wonders about the almost complete unanimity of the biographers about 8th January, and a possible reason for this error—if error it is—appears in *Aris*. In the issue dated 9th January it carried, as the first item of its column of Birmingham news, the following:

Early Yesterday Morning died in an Apopletic Fit, Mr Samuel Aris, Printer of this paper.

A number of London papers re-printed this item during the following week, and it may well be that the date of Samuel Aris's death and the date of John Baskerville's death have become confused. They were both printers; they both lived in Birmingham; both died in January 1775.

7

During this year, 1775, one book appeared "Printed by Sarah Baskerville". It was *An Introduction to the Knowledge of Medals*, by the late Rev. David Jennings, D.D., second edition . . . The production may well have been begun by Baskerville and completed by his widow, or Robert Martin, after his death.

Only one other book was "printed by Sarah Baskerville": an edition of Horace's works in 1777. That this book appeared at all is most surprising, for Sarah had clearly stated, only a month or two after Baskerville's death, that she was giving up the printing side of the business.

In 1775, and again in 1777, type-specimen sheets were issued.[1] They contain a nearly complete range of Baskerville types and all the ornaments he ever used.

The visit of Lichtenberg, referred to earlier, also took place in 1775. He was Professor of Physics at Gottingen, and an Anglophile, who made his first visit to England in 1770. His second visit, lasting for over twelve months, took place in the years 1774–5, and during that time he wrote fairly regularly to Dieterich, a well-known publisher and bookseller. Fairly soon after he arrived he wrote:

Kew, 30 Oct 1774

My dear Dieterich,

. . . Now I will tell you what the King said of your printing [of the works of Mayer] in his own words: "that is excellent printing, worthy, indeed of the man's writings", he said immediately he opened it, "as good as Baskerville."[2]

[1] Gaskell xvi. [2] M. & Q.: p. 59.

Lichtenberg was also an admirer of Baskerville's printing. He came to Birmingham the next year and again wrote to Dieterich:

St. Paul's Coffee House, London
13 Oct 1775

My dear Dieterich,

. . . Chiefly to oblige you, I journeyed to Birmingham, which is more than 24 German miles distant, purposely to converse with Mr. Baskerville. Only on my arrival there did I learn that he was buried more than six months ago. I waited on his widow, an excellent woman, who is continuing the type-foundry, but has almost entirely given up the printing-press [see p. 13]. . . . She gave me six samples of her specimens of type and quoted the prices per pound. When she discovered that I was a great admirer of her husband, she presented me, taking up from her table, with the prayer-book about which I lately wrote to you and which can no longer be obtained in Lon. She assured me that she had other prayer-books, besides some unbound copies of her husband's edition. If I or any one else in Germany wish to purchase type, she is always willing to send it post free to London as soon as I communicate with her, which is no trifle in this expensive country. Although she was dressed very nicely in black silk, she accompanied me herself into all the most dirty nooks of the type-foundry. I saw the punches and matrices for all the elegant letters which we have so often admired [see pp. 40–1] . . . Another secret of which she is as proud as she is of the glazing is the receipt of her husband's printer's ink, which is unknown to all English printers. It differs not only in the beauty of the colour, but because it dries extraordinarily quickly and is absorbed by a glazed surface much better and sooner than the common variety.

Since she herself takes no pleasure in such a life and is rich enough, she is willing to sell her whole printing equipment, with all punches, matrices, and everything appertaining to the type-foundry, besides the glazing machine and the receipt for printer's ink, for £4,000, her husband formerly having been offered £5,000 for all this; she will either give 5 per cent discount on the £4,000 for immediate payment, or six months' credit, and make free delivery to London. She has not yet advertised her intentions in black and white and not a soul is aware of them beyond her own relations and friends in Birmingham. What a chance, if only one had the money; Just fancy the type that might be cast from the existing moulds and the moulds that might be struck with the existing punches; It is a transaction which would either make a man's fortune or bankrupt him. I scarcely think it would do for Germany and, although she promised me not to be in too great haste to advertise the matter publicly, I apprehend that this will occur before we could come to any decision; then it will certainly either remain in England or go to Holland, where she has lately sold type for £150 . . .[1]

Lichtenberg also mentioned his visit in a letter to another of his correspondents, saying that Sarah had entertained him with Madeira and toast.[2]

Sarah may have told her visitor that she had no intention of advertising her plans of selling off the printing equipment, but she had, in fact, already advertised that she was giving up the printing side of the business and was proposing merely to continue as a type-founder. In an advertisement in *Aris* dated 21st August, 1775, she had said:

Baskerville Types

The late Mr. Baskerville having taken some Pains to establish a new and perfect Letter Foundry for the more readily casting of Printing Types for Sale; and as the Undertaking was finished but little Time before his Death, it is now become necessary for his Widow, Mrs. Baskerville, to inform all Printers, that she continues in the same Business, and has now ready for Sale, A Large Stock of Types of most sizes, cast with all possible Care, and dressed with the utmost Accuracy. She hopes the acknowledged Partiality of the World, in regard to the peculiar Beauty of Mr. Baskerville's Types in the Works he has published, will render it quite unnecessary here to say any Thing to recommend them, only that she is determined to attend to the Undertaking with all possible Care and Dilligence; and to the End that so

[1] M. & Q.: pp. 94–5.   [2] M. & Q.: p. 98.

useful an Improvement may become as extensive as possible, and not withstanding the great Advantage to the Buyer, in Regard to the extraordinary Hardness and Durability of these Types before all others, she will conform to sell them at the same Price with other Letter-Founders.

As Mrs Baskerville totally declines the Printing Business the Presses, cases, chases, and whole Apparatus belonging to the Printing-Office, will be disposed of in a short time, of which proper Notice will be given in a future paper.

This is the first of a series of advertisements and negotiations intended to sell off firstly the printing apparatus, secondly the book stock, and finally the type-founding equipment, which went on for the next few years.

Sometime after this date, Sarah must have been in touch with Matthew Boulton to use his London agent Motteux to make contact with Paris to see if there was any possibility of disposing of equipment and material there, because Motteux wrote to Boulton from London on 30th November, 1775:

> The particulars of Mrs Baskerville's types, etc. together with a specimen of their printing has been forwarded to a person at Paris, much connected with the rich Booksellers there. Her offer is under consideration and if it should meet with approbation you shall immediately be advised of it. With foreign ministers there is a poor chance of success and the certainty of great trouble.[1]

and on 11th December he wrote again:

> We send you copy of our Paris friend's letter, and after perusal desire you will comply immediately with what he wishes; he begs the two setts of each author may be charged at the lowest price, as they are specimens for the booksellers. He also wants to know the quantity of each book and if a long credit can be given by Mrs Baskerville to any very safe purchasers who would contract for the whole or for a large parcel. The French booksellers are always allowed very long credits

[1] Bennett: II, p. 53.

by their own countrymen. As they seem to treat seriously in this business every one of their queries should be answered distinctly and expeditiously.

We are, etc.

J. Motteux & Co.

The letter Motteux enclosed was:

Agreeable to what I had the pleasure to write you in my letter of 27th Nov. I had last Saturday a conversation of near two hours with the person who conducts at present the first foundry of printing characters at this place relative to the stock of the late Mr. Baskerville. He has given me every means I could wish for to dispose of it here and told me how to apply to the Minister for as I had foreseen it nobody but the King can make a purchase of ye kind and the Ministers to whom I must apply are luckily great admirers of Typographical performances. I shall accordingly deliver them this week two memorials I have ready for them, but as in all probability they'll appoint somebody of the profession to examine the particulars of my proposal I want details which I must beg of you to procure me as soon as possible from the widow or the person who conducted the foundry and the presses under the inspection of Mr Baskerville. You have sent me a specimen of the different characters. I want two or three more, even half a dozen, if some friend was coming over to bring them. The memorandum of the punches, matrices and moulds I understand perfectly well, and I suppose the numbers means the quantity of pieces that compose each letter. Pray inquire into it. You do not say what quantity of letters there is left, of what kind, their condition, and if they are to make part of the purchase. They sell them here by weight, and fetch little when they have been worked. Pray give me all the particulars you can relative to that article. Mr Baskerville had a particular kind of ink and paper, the glazing of the last in particular was as much admired as his character. I suppose the composition of those articles was a secret; has he transmitted it to his widow, and does it make part of her bargain? Another thing which was also much admired was the neatness of his Editions. I apprehend that depended much on his workmen, but it may also be that he had some particular proceedings in the execution. To treat with the Minister or the person he'll name I shall want all these particulars to be able to conclude at once, and I shall leave you the arbitrator of the compensation of my trouble if I succeed, for if I do not I shall think myself sufficiently rewarded by my endeavours to serve one of your friends. The only favour I beg is that in case of any foreign applications from this country to Mrs Baskerville, that she will not hearken to them, but refer them to me, and you know me well enough to assure her that her confidence will not be misplaced. As to the different Editions that remain of Mr Baskerville's Classicks, they form a separate article for which I am in treaty with a very capital Bookseller, You must be so kind to send me by way of Calais two setts of each author in a case.[1]

All these documents are in the collection at the Birmingham Assay Office, and there is also another, undated, which appears to be the draft of an answer to the request from Paris. It is a single sheet of paper, folded once. On the first page appears information about the numbers of Baskerville's classics still in stock and about discounts, type and ink:

	Nº. of Copies		
Terence	850 ⎫		
Catullus	780 ⎬ 4º		at 10/6
Lucretius	800 ⎪		
Sallust & Florus	850 ⎭		
Juvenal & Persius	250	4º	at 6/6
Terence	1000 ⎫		
Catullus	800 ⎬ 12mo		2/3
Lucretius	980 ⎪		
Sallust & Florus	800 ⎭		
Virgil	680	8vo Small	at 2/6

N.B. The Quartos lately reduced from 12/– to 10/6 and the Duodecimos from 2/6 to 2/3. Virgil from 3/– to 2/6. The usual Credit given to Booksellers here is 6, 9 & 12 months when the purchase is considerable.

[1] Bennett: II, pp. 54–5.

The Quantity of Letter on hand is almost one Hundred weight of each size, quite new, has never been touch'd with Ink. The method of making printing Ink to be communicated to the Purchaser.

The person who wrote that continues on the second page with:

As to Glazing it is an Advantageous branch of Business at present in post paper; therefore shou'd make a separate article; but if they choose it it shall be had on very easy Terms.

At this point another person has written: "—the Glazing of ye paper & ye Composition of ye Ink hath always been kept a secret but they may have it."

And the second person continues, much less literately, making points as they occur to him rather than in the order in which, one hopes, they appeared in the letter despatched to Motteux:

Mrs Baskervill hath ye very honest man which performed all ye manual opperations both in respect of fileing ye punchions, making ye letter moulds & every other improvement which Mr Baskervill made in printing He hath worked with Mr Baskervill upwards of 28 years & is articled to ye Widow for Life. She is willing to resign ye Man with all or any part of his Contract to the purchaser of ye punchions & that without any fee or other consideration as this Man can manage both ye making of original punchions the foundry ye paper & every thing I think he would be useful to ye purchaser for it w^d be necessary they should send a person to be instructed or take ye afores^d man.

The aforesaid is the last reduced price as sold to the London Booksellers but if the purchaser chooses to take ye whole M^{rs} B will make him a further reduction of 10 p^r Cent.

It was Mr Baskervills custom to melt the Types when they had completed One Book so that he always printed wth new Letter.

Mrs Baskervill says she hath fonts of New Letter never Inked of all ye sizes ready made up for Sale as she intended to keep on ye business of ye foundry provided she had not sold the punchions. She hath not taken a distinct inventory of them but guesses that she hath ab £400 worth of Type ready made up for sale.

Mrs Baskervill hath adv^{td} (see ye Birm^g Gazett) to sell all ye implements of ye printing office such as ye printing presses, the Cases &c, but as she desirous of giving the refuse of every thing belonging to ye s^d office to ye purchasers of the punches she therefore will postpone ye sale untill an answer can be recv^d from your friend at Paris, As these presses &c are more accurately made than other printers it perhaps would be proper to purchase them as they will not come to more than £14 a piece wth ye Iron Chases.

Be assured that Mrs Baskerv will not enter into treaty with any person of this or any other country untill your friend hath made his final conclusion even if they sh^d offer more than she asks M^{rs} B hath sent by this day's Wagon a Box containing agreeable to ye request of y^r friend 2 Setts of each of ye Classiks.

Sarah had indeed advertised in the *Birmingham Gazette*. In the issue dated 11th December 1775:

Baskerville's Printing Office

To be sold by Auction on the Premises by Thomas Warren, on Wednesday the 3rd of January, 1776, All the Printing Materials belonging to the late Mr John Baskerville, at Easy-Hill, Birmingham; consisting of Four accurate improved Printing Presses; several large Fonts of Types, different Sizes; with Cases, Frames, screwed Chases, and every other useful Apparatus in that Branch of Trade.—Catalogues of which will be distributed in due Time, and may be had of the Auctioneer in Dale-End, Birmingham.—The Sale will begin exactly at Ten o'clock in the Morning.

Mrs Baskerville continues the Letter Foundry as usual; and humbly hopes that the great Improvements Mr Baskerville has been universally allowed to have made in that important Business will procure her the Favours of an indulgent Public, at the usual Prices heretofore established in the Trade.

And she repeated the advertisement on 18th December, but she kept her word to postpone the auction, for the following advertisement appeared on 25th December:

Baskerville's Printing Office.
Advertised to be disposed of the 3rd January, 1776, is postponed to a
future Day, of which proper Notice will be given in this and other
public papers.

The next letter from Motteux to Boulton is dated 26th February,
1776:

I cannot give you by any other means so good a relation of the progress making at Paris for the disposal of Mrs Baskerville's printing
apparatus etc. as by sending you the original letters and papers
received from thence on that subject which you will find here enclosed.
Pray examine and consider the whole matter well and then give me
the best information you can which shall be immediately transmitted.
You know to treat with a Court and particularly such a Court as that
of France, there are many engines to be set at work and that all the
wheels of such engines will turn heavily unless they are well oiled.
Great progress is already made in the business and probably it will
proceed, if it does my friend Perregaux will have much merit and
must be well rewarded. I throw out this that Mrs Baskerville may not
expect more than she has asked, if quite so much notwithstanding
larger sums are spoken of in the memorials. Pray take care she does
not communicate with anybody whatever on this matter before she
has an affirmative or negative answer through you, probably she will
have some underhand applications thro' other channels, to which she
must absolutely turn a deaf ear, or overset everything already done.
The negotiations will not be tedious, considering there are innumer-
able forms of office to go through, before any bargain is finally con-
cluded. It is a great matter, that some of the principal officers of state
approve the purchase on the King's account. You will observe that
should the French Ministry not close there is a chance of closing with
the booksellers of Paris, on the whole Mrs B. must be cautious in mentioning the affair and avoid treating with any person whatever till a
final answer comes from France. I think you will not be amiss to give
me two letters, the one ostensible speaking of the price &c. as Mr
Perregaux states it, the other that may serve him as a guide for him-

self. I know you wish to render Mrs Baskerville service which makes me trouble you without any apology on the subject.[1]

What Sarah, or Boulton who was almost certainly advising her in the affair, thought of this we cannot tell; but we must assume that the letter, or the accompanying papers which are not extant, decided her that the French venture was not worth pursuing. In *Aris* for 11th March, 1776 there is an advertisement for type, phrased exactly as her advertisement of 21st August, 1775,[2] but it concludes with these words: "... the Presses, Cases, Chases, and whole Apparatus belonging to the Printing-Office, with a large Quantity of Types, little if at all the worse for wear will be disposed of by public Auction on Tuesday the second of April next". The advertisement was repeated for the next three weeks.

Presumably Pearson, who was now the printer of *Aris's Birmingham Gazette*, bought some type at the sale, for the issue of the paper dated 15th April (not quite a fortnight afterwards) has a paragraph asking subscribers in the area to the north-east of Birmingham to get in touch with the proprietors as the agent for the paper in that area had died and left his accounts in disorder. The announcement is set in Baskerville's Long Primer roman and italic, although one line of capitals is set in a different face—probably a Caslon.

Pearson used the type again on 24th June to announce a rise in the cost of the paper. Obviously he used the type in the paper only for this sort of announcement, to emphasise it; and the use of Baskerville's type certainly has this effect. Larger than the text-type of the paper, and infinitely more elegant, it stand out as if spot-lighted—even though, by Baskerville standards, it is shockingly inked and printed. And from this time onwards, a number of printers were using authentic Baskerville type regularly, either bought at the sale or from Sarah who continued to cast type and sell it, to judge from her advertisements.

There was a final flurry of the French venture early in 1777. On 4th February, a bookseller at the "Chateau à Versailles" called Brunet wrote to "Monsieur Baskerville". This is a translation of the letter:

[1] Bennett: II, pp. 57–8.
[2] see pp. 136–7.

I have the honour of sending you this letter hoping to gain your confidence and to make purchases of English books from you. I do not doubt that you will be surprised at the proposal, as I have not the honour of being known by you, but the details of my letter will, without difficulty, prove to you that you may be assured of my probity, and if I take the liberty of approaching you without preliminaries, it is because it is in my interest to get books direct and not to pay any middle-man; in addition I shall have the double advantage of the honour of knowing you. If this affair interests you, I flatter myself that you will tell me what means you use so that your goods arrive at the correct address and what is your method of dealing with the payments made to you so that I may conform; will you be good enough to enclose your catalogue with your answer. Here are the names of people in France from whom you can get references about me . . .

                 I have the honour to await your reply &c

The translation reflects the document[1] from which it is taken: it is a copy, presumably made in Motteux's office, by someone to whom the niceties of the French language were not over-familiar. On the back is written, in the same hand:

On the other side is a Copy of a Letter transmitted by Mrs Baskerville: She wishes to know if the treaty Mr Perregaux had kindly commenced last year for the Sale of her Types &c^a is totally at an End or not, & she farther request the favour of an Information whether Mr Brunet is a person of such Character and Solidity, as ought to induce her to trust him. If Mr Perregaux can answer these questions Mr M. would be much obliged to him for doing it; he also desires to know if Books can be entered at Calais on payment of small Duty, or if the duty is high? The Latin Classics such as Terence, Catullus, Sallust, Lucretius, Juvinal, Horace & Virgil may be admissable but he supposes that Shaftesbury's & Milton's Works & Common Prayer Books cannot.

On the bottom half of this side of the sheet of paper is written, in a quite different hand:

[1] In the Birmingham Assay Office.

Brunet au Chateau à Versailles passes amongst ye booksellers here to be a good man, But I should not chuse to trust him above Louis 1200—

I have no more hopes to succeed here in ye disposal of Mrs Baskerville's stock, they vanished with Mr Turgot's retreat, he was ye only man under whose aegis I could expect to succeed.

The duty on Books is removed & all ye above works could easily go to Versailles—

There is no Chambre Syndicale there. My best Compliments wait on Mr Motteux.

It is a fair assumption that at this point Sarah gave up her attempts to sell in France the remaining books and what remained of the printing equipment. Fairly soon afterwards she sold the remaining book stock to William Smart, a bookseller in Worcester,[1] though Straus and Dent say she sold them "a few months after Baskerville's death . . . for £1100."[2]

The matter is not made any clearer by Dibdin who said:

. . . Respecting the Prayer Books of Baskerville, the late Mr. Smart, bookseller at Worcester, (who died a very old man) told me, about ten or twelve years ago, that on the death of that printer he made the best of his way to Birmingham, and purchased of his widow all the copies of the Prayer Books which remained, together with a considerable number of the Horace of 1762.[3]

and, writing of Baskerville's *Virgil*:

. . . The late Mr. Smart, bookseller of Worcester, had probably more copies of this edition, as well as of *all* the works of Baskerville, than any other bookseller in the Kingdom.[4]

Some of the books, possibly from Smart, finished up in the hands of a J. Robson, for he advertised in *Aris* on 8th November 1784:

Baskerville's Classics

J. Robson, Bookseller, in New Bond-street, having just purchased the

[1] Bennett: II, p. 64.   [2] S. & D.: p. 128.
[3] Dibdin: *Library Companion*, pp. 48–9 note.
[4] Dibdin: *Classics* II, pp. 557–8.

very few remaining Copies of the following beautiful and elegant Editions of the Quarto Classics, printed by the late Mr Baskerville, of Birmingham, upon the finest writing royal paper, viz.

Catullus etc   Terentius

Lucretius   Sallustius

offers them to the Public at the low Price of One Pound Sixteen Shillings, the four Volumes, neatly sewed in marbled Paper—The Sale upon these Conditions to continue only for a short Time, after which they will be advanced to the original Price of One Guinea each, or disposed of abroad, from whence considerable Orders are already received.

He has also purchased the few remaining Copies of the beautiful and elegant Edition of CHARACTERISTICS by the Earl of Shaftesbury, 3 Vols, 8vo, royal Paper, with elegant Plates by Gribelin, Price only 10s. 6d. originally published at One Guinea ...

As the ingenious Artist is now no more, and his whole Apparatus, Invention of Types, and Improvement in the Art of Printing, for ever lost to this Country, the curious and lovers of Fine Books, are respectfully reminded that this is the last Opportunity they will ever have of completing their Sets of Books by this eminent Printer, or of having in their Possession Works of Elegance, which have long been the Admiration of Literati throughout Europe.

And that is very nearly all we know about the last years of Sarah's life. We do know that she lent money to Matthew Boulton, for there are receipts for interest ("28th December 1782. Received of Mr Bolton £25 for 6 Months Interest of one thousand pound") in the collection at the Birmingham Assay Office; and in 1779 Beaumarchais approached her to acquire the whole of the remaining printing and typefounding equipment:

By a deed of sale signed on 11 December 1779, the purchaser wrote that he became possessed "not only of Baskerville's letter-foundry, but also his methods of glazing paper, compounding ink; and all his other improvements, as well in the foundry as in the printing branches".[1]

[1] Dreyfus: *The Library*, p. 30.

Beaumarchais was buying all this on behalf of the Literary and Typographical Society, and Talbot Baines Reed quotes from the *St. James Chronicle*, 4th June 1782:

There appeared also *Proposals* for printing by Subscription a Complete Edition of the Works of Voltaire, printed with the Types of Baskerville for the Literary and Typographical Society 1782. 12pp 8vo with 4pp specimens of the type. The French proposal appears to have been put forward in 1780.[1]

Sarah died on 21st March, 1788. Her death was announced in *Aris* of 24th March:

On Friday, at her home on Easy-Hill, near this town, Mrs Baskerville, relict of the last Mr John Baskerville so justly celebrated for his beautiful types, and other elegant improvements in the art of printing.

She was buried in St Philip's churchyard. Her grave is a few yards from the north-east corner of the church, still clearly marked by a stone which is not the original. The present stone was substituted for the original which had, by the Second World War, deteriorated very badly. It was placed on the wall of the staircase leading from the north entrance of the church to the gallery, but parts of its legend—"In Memory of Sarah Baskerville who died March 21st 1788 aged 80 Wife of John Baskerville Printer"—are completely indecipherable.

[1] TBR: p. 286, note 2.

8

Easy Hill was sold to John Ryland on 19th May, 1788. He paid £3000 for the house, outbuildings and the lease; he had already bought the freehold of the property. He was living there in 1791 when the house was attacked and wrecked during the Birmingham Riots. After that he moved and the grounds were gradually taken over for canal wharves and buildings associated with them. One of the men concerned in this activity was a Thomas Gibson. The "conical building", in a vault of which Baskerville had been buried (presumably under the building), was demolished but the body was left undisturbed.

So it remained, until 1820 when it was discovered. The account that follows is taken from Langford:

Disinterment of Mr Baskerville.
May 28th, 1821.—It is in the recollection of many of the inhabitants of this place that Mr John Baskerville, celebrated for the improvement he made in letter-founding, was buried, by an express direction contained in his will, in his own ground, in a mausoleum erected for the purpose previous to his decease. Upon his death the ground was sold, and passed into the hands of John Ryland, Esq., and from him to his son, Samuel Ryland, Esq., who, a few years ago, demised it to Mr Gibson for a long term who has since cut a canal through it, and converted the remainder into wharf land. Soon after Mr Ryland became the possessor of this property, the mausoleum, which was a small conical building, was taken down, and, it was rumoured at the time, that the body had been removed.

This proved, however, to be unfounded, for it appears that a short time before Christmas last, some workmen, who were employed in getting gravel, discovered the leaden coffin. It was however immediately covered up, and remained untouched until a few days since, when, the spot having been recently let for a wharf, it became necessary to remove the coffin, and it was accordingly disinterred, and deposited in Messrs. Gibson and Son's warehouse, where a few individuals were allowed to inspect it. The body was in a singular state of preservation, considering that it had been under ground about 46 years. It was wrapt in a linen shroud, which was very perfect and white, and on the breast lay a branch of laurel, faded, but entire, and firm in texture. There were also leaves, and sprigs of bay and laurel in other parts of the coffin and on the body. The skin on the face was dry but perfect. The eyes were gone, but the eyebrows, eyelashes, lips and teeth remained. The skin on the abdomen and body generally was in the same state with that of the face. An exceedingly offensive and oppressive effluvia, strongly resembling decayed cheese, arose from the body, and rendered it necessary to close the coffin in a short time, and it has since been consigned to his surviving connexions for the purpose of re-interment. It was first supposed, by those who examined the body, that some artificial means had been employed to protect it from putrefaction, but, on enquiry, it was not ascertained that this was the case. The putrefactive process must have been arrested by the leaden coffin having been sealed hermetically, and thus the access of air, which modern discoveries have ascertained is essential to putrefaction, was prevented.[1]

In spite of that report, it seems that the coffin was left in Gibson's warehouse for the next eight years. Bennett quotes a letter from someone who lived next door to the warehouse in Cambridge Street where it is alleged that Gibson used to charge 6d. a head "to see the body . . . and as a child I saw the coffin reared upon end in Gibson's . . ."[2] In August 1829 it was transferred to the shop of John Marston, a plumber and

[1] Langford: II, pp. 358–9.
[2] Bennett: II, pp. 77–8.

glazier, who lived in Monmouth Street at just about the point where was later constructed the entrance to the old Snow Hill station.

The coffin was again opened and a local artist, Thomas Underwood, made a pencil sketch of the body. The sketch is preserved in the Birmingham Library, Margaret Street, and is not a pleasant sight. It is mounted in a large album of engravings, cuttings, etc. illustrating aspects of Birmingham life. On the same page is mounted what is allegedly a piece of Baskerville's shroud and by it is mounted a piece of paper on which are the words "Relic of Mr John Baskerville taken Augt 15, 1829". Thomas Underwood also wrote an account of how he came to make the sketch:

> This sketch was taken when the remains lay at Marston's the plumber in Monmouth Street (within a few doors of which I was then an apprentice with Mr Josiah Allen, the engraver), where they were on view for some days, and were seen by a number of persons, amongst others by Dr Male and his daughter, who lived at the top of Newhall Street. The effluvium made them ill, and I believe they were laid up for some time with fever. A surgeon in Newhall Street also went, who tore a piece from the shroud, which he incautiously put into his coat pocket and died in a few days. The only ill effect upon myself, who was there upwards of an hour, was a distaste for food for several days. The body was much decomposed, but the teeth were perfect; and the sketch shows correctly what I saw of the remains of the man who was an artist in every sense of the word, and will ever deservedly be famous as one of the worthies of our town, who spread its fame the wide world over.

There were a number of such stories, told at this time and subsequently, of people who fell ill after seeing the corpse. Two more cuttings from a contemporary Birmingham newspaper (*The Birmingham Journal*) continue the story:

> August 22nd: Baskerville—It appears as if the corpse of this celebrated type founder was never to find a resting place, during the week the body having been again exposed to view. We are surprised

that no member or descendant of the family has interfered, and secured these remains in some cemetery.

September 5th: Baskerville—The remains of this singular but celebrated man (after an exhumation of seven years) have been buried once more, in a piece of ground adjoining Cradley Chapel, the property of a branch of Baskerville's family.

This latter story was untrue, but was believed by many. What is probably the most nearly correct story (and certainly a most attractive one) is that told in a letter to the *Birmingham Weekly Post* of November 22nd, 1879. The letter was written by a W. J. Scofield:

For some years before her death, which occurred about eight or nine years ago, I had the pleasure of the intimate acquaintance of Mrs Marston, widow of a Mr Marston, plumber, of Monmouth Street, to whom reference has been frequently made in connection with the opening of Baskerville's coffin . . . She repeated to me more than once the history of the exhumation and burial of Baskerville's body, and I offer you her narrative. After the disinterment the body lay for a *long* time under the iron in Mr Gibson's warehouse, and was afterwards moved to Mr Marston's shop, where, as related by your other correspondents, it was opened at the suggestion of Dr Male, then a physician of note living at the top of Newhall Street, with results so disastrous that the curiosity of the town turned to alarm, and the body which Mrs Marston saw "mummied, looking but very little changed but soon changing much", was a great trouble to Mr Marston, and he was anxious to be rid of it. Having a vault at St Philip's—where he and his wife now sleep—he applied to the rector for permission for its burial there, but it was refused on account of Baskerville's "atheism"; and the difficulty continued until Mr Knott, or Nott, a bookseller, called on Mr Marston and told him he had a vault in Christ Church, and that he should consider it a great honour for Baskerville's remains to rest in it. Mr Barker, a solicitor of eminence, well known to florists as a collector of orchids, and an intimate friend of Mr Marston's, was then churchwarden of Christ Church, and to him Mr Marston applied for the requisite leave. On hearing the request, Mr Barker, with an unmistakeable twinkle of the eye, told Mr Marston it was impossible —"indeed, I keep the keys and at such time of the day they are on the hall table". Mr Marston was not slow to take the hint, and called. The door was opened by the butler, and there were the keys. Mr Marston asked if Mr Barker was at home; the servant said "No", faced about and walked off. Mr Marston took the keys, and the body in its reclosed lead coffin was carried "on a hand barrow covered with a green baize cloth", to its last resting place in Mr Nott's vault in Christ Church, and there it would doubtless now be found. I believe— but of this I am not quite certain—that a notice was inserted in a Birmingham paper a few days after, saying that the body had been buried between two pools near Netherton, beyond Dudley, on some property formerly belonging to Baskerville.

(Christ Church was at the corner of the present Colmore Row and New Street in Victoria Square, about two or three hundred yards from Easy Hill.)

The doubt most people seem to have had about where Baskerville's body had been put was not surprising. In Volume VIII of Nichols, published in 1858, there is a copy of a letter written in 1829 which describes the body being in Marston's warehouse and repeats the story of the burial at Cradley.[1] But in Notes & Queries, 1851,[2] there is a note from William Cornish of Birmingham which categorically states "the body of the eminent printer now reposes, as it has for some years, in the vault of Christ Church in our town".

In 1892 Talbot Baines Reed suggested, at a lecture in Birmingham about Baskerville, that the mystery ought really to be solved. One of the churchwardens of Christ Church made a check of the burial records of the church and discovered that although there were 136 vaults under the church, only 135 burials were recorded. As a result of this, and under pressure from a number of interested local people, the vault was opened. A very full account was given in the *Birmingham Daily Argus* of 12th April, 1893:

[1] Nichols: *Illustrations* VIII, p. 458.
[2] N. & Q., 1st Series, Vol IV, p. 211.

Such a gathering as that which assembled in Christ Church this morning and went down on a journey of discovery into the catacombs below is unique . . . Mr Albert Taylor, one of the churchwardens, had previously examined the registers and searched the catacombs . . . there was one filled in that had no description, and instead of a stone slab, the mouth of the vault was filled in with brickwork. If Baskerville was buried in the catacombs, in this vault his remains would be found. In the register this vault was numbered 521, and it belonged to Mr George Barker, who was a solicitor in the town and one of the churchwardens of Christ Church in 1829. The Vicar, Canon Wilcox, acquiesced in the suggestion that this vault should be opened this morning in the presence of the Mayor . . . and others . . . Before descending to the catacombs Canon Wilcox said there was nothing in the register to prove that the vault was ever transferred from Mr Barker, or that anyone was buried in it, and that was the reason why they felt at liberty to interfere with it. If they did find a coffin, and the medical faculty approved, they proposed to open it and then have it properly cemented up in the vault and an inscription tablet placed on it and also *perhaps* in the church . . . The gathering then went down into the arch of the catacombs and, packed together, with their hats touching the roof, waited in silence the removal of the brickwork and cement by two workmen. When the first layer had been chiselled and sawn out, another lot was exposed to view underneath. This was regarded by some as ominous, because, if the coffin was behind it must be an extremely small one. On the other hand, another section argued that it was favourable to the theory that there was a coffin surreptitiously placed there. Two bricks were knocked away from the second row and one of the workmen, putting his hand through, said he could feel a coffin. By means of a reflector wall lamp, which lighted the vault, it could be seen that the coffin was of lead, and as the next two bricks came out, on the head was seen in printing types, soldered on, "John Baskerville". Underneath the type, in chalk, was written "Removed in 1829", and over the top, less distinctly, "Died 1775". On the lead coffin being drawn out it was found to be very short, 5 feet 6 inches, and proportionately narrow. The lead was opened and underneath were four pieces of oak, very rotten but dry. On these being removed the body was exposed to view, with a quantity of matting dividing it from the lead sides. There was no inner wooden coffin and the brown shroud was pinked at the edges . . . The skull and overlying brown skin were intact, the jaw was firm and the skull massive. Mr Timmins unhesitatingly decided the remains to be those of Baskerville, answering in every description to portraits in his possession. Dr Rickards and Professor Windle closely examined the body. The former said "it was not surprising the skeleton should be in that condition, but he was surprised it did not crumble to dust on exposure." The coffin was quickly closed up again, deposited in the vault and cemented in. Prior to this, photographs and tracings of the inscription were taken . . .

The affair caused a considerable amount of local interest and, indeed, a question was asked about the legality of the affair in Parliament. The *Birmingham Post* of 18th April carried a leader on the subject: a fine example of outraged Victorian propriety, but the perpetrators could not have felt much shame for their actions, for according to Walker a tablet bearing the following inscription was placed soon afterwards on the outside wall of Christ Church:

In these catacombs rest the remains of

John Baskerville

The famous printer

He died in 1775, but the place of his burial was unknown until April 12th 1893, when the opening of the unregistered catacomb No. 521 disclosed a coffin, which on further examination was found to contain his body; the remains were left intact, and the coffin was replaced in the catacomb and the proper entry made in the burials register by the Vicar.

There were present

Alderman Lawley Parker, Mayor

Oliver Pemberton, M.D., Coroner, F.R.C.S.

A. Hill, M.D., Medical Officer

W. S. Till, Esq., City Surveyor

Sam. Timmins, Esq.
T. H. Ryland, Esq.,
Representatives of the local press and others
Charles Byron Wilcox, Vicar
Albert Taylor ⎱ Churchwardens
William Gay ⎰
This tablet was erected by public subscription.

That, however, is not the end of the story. Christ Church was consecrated in 1813 when Birmingham was expanding rapidly westwards
from its original centre in the direction of Easy Hill, in fact. By the 1890s,
the area round the church had changed from being residential and was
becoming, as it is now, the administrative and professional centre of the
town. The church of St. Philip, only two or three hundred yards away
along Colmore Row, was easily large enough to cope with the declining
number of people who lived in the area. In 1897, an Act was passed in
spite of considerable local opposition to authorise the demolition of the
church and the sale of the site.

The church was demolished, and a block of shops and offices erected
on the site. This in turn was demolished two or three years ago and the
site is now grassed over; the only reminder of Christ Church is a walk
and flight of steps on the edge of the site known as Christ Church
Passage.

The bodies in the catacombs had to be removed before the church
could be demolished, and as no relatives or friends came forward to
claim Baskerville's body "it was reinterred in the Church of England
cemetery, Warstone Lane, in a vault beneath the chapel, and at the
entrance to the vault was placed the tablet from the wall of Christ
Church, with the date of its removal added 'February 26, 1898'."[1]

Warstone Lane Cemetery is set in the middle of Birmingham's jewel-
lery quarter, and was opened in the middle of the nineteenth century. It
was privately owned until the early 1950s when the city took it over. The
land falls quite steeply and the chapel was situated on the highest part,
with the entrances to the two levels of vaults beneath the chapel in a sort

[1] Walker: p. 13.

155

of excavated amphitheatre more than half way down the slope. The chapel has now been demolished and the entrances to the vaults were recently bricked up to prevent vandals and metal thieves from interfering with the graves. As a result, the tablet from Christ Church can no longer be seen.

The saga of Baskerville's body is strange enough: the story of his equipment is almost stranger. When Sarah sold it to Beaumarchais in 1779, it was in order that he should print an edition of the complete works of Voltaire. The story of this enterprise—a mixture of almost every human fault that folly and inefficiency can breed—and the subsequent history of the types is told in great detail by John Dreyfus in his long article in *The Library*.[1] The seat of the affair was at Kehl, in the principality of Baden-Durlach, but in 1790 the Baskerville punches, matrices and type were transported to Paris where much type was cast and used for printing during the revolutionary period and for the following twenty years. A certain amount of imitation Baskerville type was also produced during the same period.

In 1816 Beaumarchais' daughter sold all the remaining Baskerville equipment (it was now reduced merely to the type-founding apparatus) to the firm of Didot, who offered it in 1819 to Francis Henry Egerton, later Earl of Bridgewater. He refused, and in 1838 it was sold to the firm of Plon Frères, who in turn sold it to the firm of A. Bertrand in the 1890s. Plon made it one of the conditions of the sale that Bertrand should supply them with type and they used type made from the original punches to print a book published in 1907: *La Terence des Ducs* by Henry Martin.

As Dreyfus points out, this book was printed in the year Straus and Dent published the first account of John Baskerville's life and work to be written—it was printed in Caslon type at the Cambridge University Press. And even more remarkable, it was an American who finally recognised the true nature of the "elzévirs anciens" as Bertrand called them. Bruce Rogers, the greatest of all American typographers, wrote in 1944, in an appendix to the second edition of Benton[2] that he saw a prospectus of a book published in Paris by Plon, Nourrit & Cie, set in a

[1] Dreyfus: *The Library*, pp. 26–48.
[2] Benton: 2nd ed., pp. 100–1.

Baskerville which looked like the real thing and when he enquired about it was told they had bought it from a foundry which had gone out of business. When he joined the Harvard University Press he managed to persuade Plon, Nourrit & Cie to cast a fount of Baskerville for use by the Press at Harvard. The first book printed in Baskerville at the Press was a folio edition of *The Cemetery at Sousain,* published in 1921. He used it for another six books while he was at Harvard.

Dreyfus takes up the story with the information that Bertrand sold all their foundry material to Deberny and Peignot in 1936: it included 2,750 punches and 3,052 matrices for making Baskerville type. He carefully compared these punches with the punches for Baskerville's Greek which are still kept at Oxford University Press and estimates that three-quarters of the roman punches are genuine Baskerville originals.

The final episode in this saga took place in 1953. In that year the firm of Deberny Peignot presented all the punches which they then had to the Cambridge University Press. And, even though Baskerville's association with the University of Cambridge was not entirely happy, it is difficult to think of a better place in which these much-travelled punches could have come finally to rest.

9

Fifty years ago, when the Baskerville revival (and indeed the revival of type-design) was just beginning, it was possible to argue about what was his greatest contribution to the art of printing; his press-work, his ink, his paper, or the design of his type. It is still possible to argue; but great as was the influence in their time of the other three, there can be little doubt after roughly fifty years of widely available Baskerville types that his most obvious influence in the twentieth century has been his type.

In Hugh Williamson's *Methods of Book Design* (Second Edition, London, 1966) he has a short Appendix[1] on type-face popularity. He lists the twelve type-faces most frequently appearing in the National Book League's annual exhibition—not necessarily, as he points out, "a sure index of popularity; the books are selected for their excellence of production, and are not necessarily typical, in the choice of types, of British output in general . . . but the figures may reasonably be supposed to show which types tend to be preferred by good designers when doing some of their best work."

Baskerville was used, in the 1945–55 period, for 115 books out of 823; and in 1956–63, for 111 out of 831; only Bembo was more popular.

A count of the figures in the National Book League's catalogues since the last exhibition that Williamson could cover shows that Baskerville has continued to retain its popularity. In the period 1964–73, it was used for 152 books out of 1069; and though the proportion varies slightly from year to year, there is a remarkable consistency about the figures.

[1] pp. 407–8.

For example, in 1964: 13 out of 129; 1968: 18 out of 155; 1973: 14 out of 119.

In his introduction to the second edition of Benton's book,[1] 1944, Zolton Haraszti says that in the previous year no fewer than thirteen of the annual selection of the Fifty Books of the Year by the American Institute of Graphic Arts were printed in Baskerville type.

The question of what decided Baskerville to set up as a type-designer and printer is one which cannot be answered except by the various pronouncements he made himself. It may be, as some writers have suggested, that the publication in June, 1750, of a long article on type-founding in *The Universal Magazine* may have set him off, but the desire must have been there before that date.

One can perhaps go further towards answering the question of why his types look as they do. Berry and Johnson state categorically:[2] "While Caslon ignored the 'romains du roi', it is clear that Baskerville was acquainted with the letter, as he took several details from it . . .", and "The influence of the French type designers is more obvious in Baskerville's italic than in his roman . . .", although, to be fair to them, they do also mention the influence of the writing-masters. The "romain du roi" was first discussed in 1691, was designed on mathematical bases by a committee but, fortunately, was cut by Grandjean, one of the great punch-cutters. It was made for the exclusive use of the Royal Printing House in France and was first used for a folio *Médailles sur les Principaux Evènements du Règne de Louis le Grand* . . . published in 1702. The type certainly was a break with tradition and has qualities which Baskerville's type showed half a century later.

The other popular answer to the question is the influence of the writing-masters, and in particular George Shelley, who published *Alphabets in All the Hands* about 1715. Whether Baskerville was acquainted with the "romain du roi" it is impossible to say, but it is nearly impossible that he was not acquainted with Shelley's book: it is inconceivable that any professional writing-master in the period when Baskerville was teaching writing would not have known of the book. And again, the letters in Shelley show qualities which re-appear in Baskerville's type.

[1] Benton: p. xx.   [2] B. & J.: pp. 28–9.

ABCDEFGHIJKLM

abcdefghijklmnop

ABCDEFGHIJKLMN

OPQRSTUVWXYZÆ.

qrſstuvwxyzæœ&.

Shelley Scrip.

French Cannon

NOPQRSTUWXYZ.

French Cannon.

A B C D E F G H

Tandem aliquando, Quirites!

Two-line Double Pica.

Tandem aliquando, Quirites! L. Catili-

Tandem aliquando, Quirites! L. Catilinam

Hand-drawn letters from George Shelley's *Alphabets in All the Hands* and
two of Baskerville's larger types from the 1777 type-specimen (reduced)

He, himself, of course said quite definitely in the preface to his *Milton* in 1758[1] that he wanted to contribute to the perfection of the letter and tried to produce a set of types "according to what I conceived to be their true proportion". His reference to Caslon, in that preface, is, one suspects, no more than a polite acknowledgment of his predecessor. He certainly did not base any of his designs on Caslon's.

As with so many other questions, there is no definite answer. All we know is that he did design type—and it has been there for study for over two hundred years. No one ever has been, and probably no one ever will be, able to identify definitively the sources of an artist's inspiration—or even of a craftman's original design.

The importance of the question, and the fascination of the attempt to answer it, lies almost entirely in the fact that Baskerville, in this country at least, was the innovator of a new style and tradition of type-design. If he had merely imitated Caslon, even if he had improved on him, there would have been little to say, or to speculate about; but he abandoned the Caslon tradition, and with Grandjean, Fournier and other type-cutters, began a new tradition which, during the eighteenth century, revolutionised the appearance of the printed page.

Caslon was the last of a line. The letters he cut (and he was merely a letter-cutter and founder; he did no printing) trace their shape back through the Dutch letter he imitated and refined to the Italian type-faces of the fifteenth century. For nearly two hundred years the design of the roman and italic alphabets had merely been a question of refining and improving the type-faces of the previous generation. The Caslon letter may look very different, superficially, from that used by Aldus, but essentially it is the same. In fact, Stanley Morison's book *On Type Designs* describes the illustration of Caslon it uses as "English version of the Aldine roman by William Caslon".[2]

The revolution which Grandjean, and Baskerville, brought about was in the relationship between the thick and the thin parts of the letter, in the position of the thickest part of the letter, and in the treatment of serifs. All these are minutiae; but type-design *is* a matter of minutiae.

Baskerville thickened the thick parts of his roman letter and made the

[1] see p. 61.   [2] New edition, 1962, p. 52.

Great Primer Roman.

A B C D E F G H I J
K L M N O P Q R S T
U V W X Y Z

a b c d e f g h i j k l m n o p q r s
t u v w x y z

Great Primer Italic.

A B C D E F G H I J
K L M N O P Q R S T
U V W X Y Z

a b c d e f g h i j k l m n o p q r s
t u v w x y z

1 2 3 4 5 6 7 8 9 0

Baskerville's Great Primer type. This should not be taken as a definitive alphabet: many of the ligatures he used are not shown; and many of the letters exist in various forms—for example, Baskerville used at least three versions of the italic capital *K* (two being shown in the same line on p. 87 of Shaftesbury's *Characteristicks*)

162

thin parts thinner, giving them a sharper, smarter appearance. He did not go as far as the later eighteenth-century designers (Bodoni being the best example) who reduced the thin parts to a hair-line and deliberately made the thick parts look swollen, but he showed them the way.

He pulled the thickest part of a curved letter away from the position of being at 45° to the horizontal and raised it higher up the curve. The effect is that given by writing with a chisel-ended pen held at 45° to the line of writing, and then held so that the pen is more nearly at right-angles to the line. Again he pointed the way for the more exaggerated designs of the later part of the century.

He made more of the serifs of the letters, making them more notice-able by giving them a sharper, spiky quality. At the end of the century the serif had become merely a hair-line, but he did not go as far as that.

These minute changes of details would probably have gone un-noticed except by the printers of the country if it had not been for his superb presswork, superior ink, and smooth paper. These high-lighted the changes he had made, and were, possibly even more than the changes themselves, responsible for the accusations of blinding the reader which were commonly made against him. Anyone who has looked at the books or pamphlets printed in Baskerville's type by other printers after his death will see how much of the effect is lost owing to inferior presswork.

Dr John Bedford who wrote to Richard Richardson in 1758, though his intention was denigratory, spoke truer than he knew:

Durham, Oct 29, 1758

Dear Sir,

. . . By Baskerville's Specimen of his types, you will percieve how much the elegance of them is owing to his paper, which he makes himself, as well as the types and his ink also; and I was informed, whenever they come to be used by common pressmen, and with common materials, they will lose of their beauty considerably. Hence, perhaps, this Specimen may become curious (when he is no more, and the types cannot be set off in the same perfection) and a great piece of vertu . . .[1]

[1] Quoted by Nichols: *Illustrations* I, p. 813.

Baskerville made other innovations in design. The type of the late seventeenth century was, on the whole, rather compressed—whether for reasons of aesthetic appeal or economy is difficult to say—but Baskerville gave his letters a rounded, open appearance. They take up a lot of room. (It is, incidentally, a striking tribute to their appeal to modern eyes that the twentieth-century versions of Baskerville are so popular when they are so relatively uneconomic to use.)

Stanley Morison, in the book quoted above,[1] describes Baskerville's italic as "wiry, thin and pinched". It is true that it does look a little thin when a word or two of the italic is set in a line of the corresponding roman, but it is not "pinched"—it has, in fact, a pleasant open appearance. The accusation of wiriness is perhaps also justified to some extent.

The traditional pre-Baskerville and Grandjean italic had descended from the Italian type of the first years of the sixteenth century; it had been modified in the two hundred years of its evolution, but essentially it took its characteristics from a hand-writing which was dependent on an inflexible chisel-ended pen for its qualities. The new italic had the continuous-line quality of the copper-engraver's burin—or the flexible sharp-pointed pen which Baskerville so obviously used in his own handwriting.

It is, too, a more regular letter than its predecessors: there is none of the variation in slope which is so characteristic of the Caslon letter, and he also expanded the letters, giving them a rounder, less angular look. But, elegant as most of the letters are, and well as they fit together (with the possible exception of the lower-case r which in some sizes often looks as if it has a hair-space inserted after it), it is a slightly monotonous face. That, like Morison's, is a subjective judgement—made by one who freely admits to a devotion to the chancery italic.

The most striking attribute of both roman and italic is its regularity. To eyes which are accustomed to modern type, which has been cut and cast by a machine, this may not appear very noticeable: it is only when one compares a page of one of Baskerville's books with a page of a book contemporary with it that this quality is really apparent. Even if one discounts all the superiority of his presswork, ink and paper, the fact still

[1] see p. 161.

remains: his type has a regularity no other type had ever possessed.

The lines in his books do not waver up and down as books printed by his predecessors and contemporaries often appear to do. This, one suspects, was due not only to inferior casting and the subsequent dressing, but to the design of the letters. Baskerville eliminated this fault: all his letters look the same height, the lower-case letters form as good a line along the top as along the bottom—and he must have insisted on a standard of precision in casting and dressing unbelievable at the time.

The type also looks even. Most of his predecessors' type, even when properly inked and printed, has a spotty appearance: some letters look heavier than others. Much of this quality was due to bad inking, but Baskerville obviously designed his letters to give the illusion of equal blackness, whether the letter had much or little metal in contact with the paper. Even his capitals do not stand out like black beacons on the page, as they do in so many books from the period. The letters, too, fit together closely: there is none of that feeling in his books that some careless compositor has slipped in a few hair-spaces in some of the words, or that the line is loosely set and showing gaps between the letters.

On the 1777 type-specimen[1] there are, if one counts roman and italic as separate founts, twenty-six sizes of type—and this is not complete (there is, for example, no showing of three of the sizes of type used on the title-page of the 1763 Bible). Yet in the specimen he issued in 1754[2] there were only seven, and of these only the Great Primer was shown in roman and italic, upper and lower case.

Not only did Baskerville add constantly to his repertoire of type-sizes, he also made changes to the types during the quarter century that he was concerned with the printing venture. Both Graham Pollard[3] and Gaskell draw attention to changes which were made. Pollard talks about the unique swash capital F shown in "Lord Shrewsbury's Case" and Gaskell draws attention to changes made in the italic capitals J, N, O, Q, R and T. Other letters, too, underwent subtle changes.

This is perhaps the culminating example of Baskerville's passionate

[1] Gaskell xvi. [2] Gaskell ii.
[3] *Fleuron* 7, pp. 155–6.

devotion to perfectionism, or—to put it in another and less flattering way—of the complete disregard for economic commonsense which bedevilled the whole of his printing and publishing career.

In spite of the British devotion to Caslon and similar letters, other type-cutters and founders realised that a change was coming in public taste and began to cater for it. The first of the imitations of Baskerville's type was that offered by Isaac Moore in 1766, usually referred to as Fry's Baskerville. Moore had been a whitesmith in Birmingham and moved to Bristol where he became manager and later partner in the type-foundry firm, established about 1764 by Fry and Pine. Fry was a doctor turned type-founder; Pine was a printer. Moore issued a specimen sheet of his types in 1766 and they are quite obviously closely modelled on Baskerville's.

They are so closely modelled as to have been responsible for a considerable amount of confusion in attribution. Possibly the best example of this is the book usually referred to as the last book printed in Baskerville's type in England: *The Treatyse of Fysshinge wyth an Angle*, re-printed in 1827 for William Pickering "with the types of John Baskerville". The book is in fact printed in Fry's Baskerville.

Alexander Wilson set up in business as a typefounder in 1742, and cut and founded type for Robert and Andrew Foulis of Glasgow. Some of his later types are perhaps not imitations of Baskerville's but are very obviously strongly influenced by them.

And the third of the important typefounders of the last third of the eighteenth century to be influenced by Baskerville—even if he was not deliberately imitating him—was William Martin, the brother of Robert Martin who was Baskerville's foreman. He must have learned his type cutting and founding at Easy Hill, and when he moved to London about 1786 he rapidly became associated with a group of publishers and printers including Bulmer and Boydell for whom he cut and founded type almost exclusively.

But Martin's types are really moving away from the authentic Baskerville original and one suspects that the continental type-designers had as much effect on Martin's design as did Baskerville. Taste in type and book-production was changing (as were methods of printing) and in the first years of the nineteenth century the new "modern" faces swept all before them.

So the Baskerville types—authentic, imitated, and influenced—passed into oblivion for more than a century. The developments of type-design and the revivals and imitations of the nineteenth century have no place in this account.

The first signs of a re-emergence were rather premature. In 1905 the Sheffield firm of Stephenson Blake and Co. acquired the type-foundry of Sir Charles Reed and Sons. This latter firm was—through purchase, amalgamation and inheritance—the owner of the remains of the Fry firm set up in 1764, and it still had the material for casting Fry's Basker-ville. In a type specimen dated December 1909, Stephenson Blake announced that they were offering this type to the printing trade. It was matched with small capitals and an italic from another source, but these have since been abandoned. In the roman, in a rather restricted number of sizes, it is in 1975 still available, and is popular for display work. Some of the original punches and matrices still exist.

The second revival was made by the American Type Founders Co. in 1915. It is obviously based on Fry's Baskerville rather than on the authen-tic type and was designed by Morris Fuller Benton. It is still available in Both roman and italic are still available. This book is set in this type.

The 1920s saw a number of revivals. Possibly the first of these was that carried out by the Monotype Corporation in this country. James Moran says that the decision had been made by January, 1923.[1] The model in this case was John Baskerville's Great Primer as used in his *Terence* of 1772. There are differences between the original and the revival—some deliberate, some imposed by the restrictions of the casting machine—but it is probably the most successful of the revivals, particularly in the italic. Both roman and italic are still available. This book is set in this type.

Shortly after this, the two German type-founders, Bauer and Stempel, issued versions of Baskerville. There is little point in discussing the Bauer face as it bears little resemblance to the original. The face produced by D. Stempel AG is a different matter. It was based on research done on the original types by Dr. Rudolf Wolf who was then Typographical

[1] In *Stanley Morison: His Typographic Achievement* (1971), pp. 86–7.

Manager of the firm and is as good in the roman as any of the revivals; the italic is perhaps not so successful. It was also made available in 1928 on German Linotype machines and is still available in the German Linotype and the Stempel versions.

The English Linotype made its version available in 1931. It was cut under the supervision of George W. Jones who had a fount of type cast by Bertrand in Paris from the original punches and matrices then in their possession and he used these as the basis of the English Linotype version. Within the limits imposed by slug-setting, it is a good revival of the original. It is still available.

The Harris Intertype Corporation began to cut their version of Baskerville in 1932. Some of the letters have obviously been distorted to meet the demands of the machines, but otherwise it is good. It is also still available in roman and italic.

The French type-founders Deberny Peignot produced a Baskerville which showed far too much contrast between thick and thin strokes really to be considered as a revival, though most of the letters were of the right shape. However, the firm has recently re-designed the face for the Lumitype photo-setting machine, and this is a much better version.

Many of the other type-faces mentioned above are also available for the various photo-setting devices made by their parent companies or associated with them, and a version of Baskerville is now available on an electric typewriter for the "cold setting" of type intended for offset litho.

So John Baskerville's type, two hundred years after his death and perhaps not quite in the form in which he designed it, is still being used. One wonders what he would think about it all, and one suspects that the witty tongue he had, and the sardonic turn of mind which seems so obvious from the Millar portrait, would have produced a suitable comment. One thing is as certain as it can be: he would have been delighted. And not only in a spirit of "I told you so". He was, as Hutton said, a good designer; but he also had an ingenious, mechanically-orientated mind, and he would have found the complexity and the precision of the modern printing-house a source of constant delight.

APPENDIX

✳❖✳❖✳❖✳❖✳❖✳❖✳❖✳❖✳❖✳❖✳❖✳❖✳❖✳❖✳

Books printed by John Baskerville

1757	Virgil: *Bucolica, Georgica et Aeneis.* 4°
1758	*Avon . . .* 4°
1758	Milton: *Paradise Lost.* 8° and 4°
1758	Milton: *Paradise Regained . . .* 8° and 4°
1759	Milton: *Paradise Lost.* 4°
1759	Milton: *Paradise Regained . . .* 4°
1759	*Pixell: *A Collection Of Songs . . .* 2°
1760	*Edwin and Emma.* 4°
1760	Milton: *Paradise Lost.* 8°
1760	Milton: *Paradise Regained . . .* 8°
1760	*The Book of Common Prayer.* 8° (Various editions)
1761	*Select Fables . . .* 8°
1761	Juvenal and Persius: *Satyrae.* 4°
1761	Congreve: *Works.* 3 vols. 8°
1761	Addison: *Works.* 4 vols. 4° (see p. 74)
1761	*An Ode Upon The Fleet . . .* 4°
1762	*The Book of Common Prayer.* 8°
1762	*The Book of Common Prayer.* 12°
1762	Horace. 12°
1762	Sternhold and Hopkins: *The Whole Book of Psalms . . .* 12°
1762	Brady and Tate: *A New Version of the Psalms . . .* 12°
1762	Gardiner: *Expedition to the West Indies.* 4° (and French version)
1763	*The Holy Bible.* 2°

* These books do not have John Baskerville's name on the title-page.

1764   *Select Fables* . . . 8º (see pp. 91, 95)
1764   Jennings: *An Introduction to the Knowledge of Medals.* 8º
1764   Dalby: *The Virtues of Cinnabar and Musk* . . . 4º (see pp. 91–2)
1765   Barclay: *An Apology for the True Christian Divinity* . . . 4º (see pp. 94–5)
1765   *A Vocabulary.* . . . 18º
1766   Virgil: *Bucolica, Georgica et Aeneis.* 8º
1766   Andrews: *The Works of Virgil, Englished.* 8º
1766   Andrews: *Odes* . . . 4º
1769   *The Holy Bible.* 2º (published in parts)
1769   Jackson: *The Beauties of Nature* . . . 8º
1769   Tyndal: *A Sermon Preached at Bromsgrove* . . . 8º
1769   **The Life and Political Writings of John Wilkes, Esq* . . . 8º
1770   Horace. 4º
1770   Lieutaud: *An Essay* . . . (see p. 118)
1770   *Philanthropos: *Grace Triumphant.* 8º
1771   Free: *The Political Songster* . . . 8º
1772   Lucretius: *De Rerum Natura.* 4º
1772   Catullus, Tibullus and Propertius: *Opera.* 4º
1772   Catullus, Tibullus and Propertius: *Opera.* 12º
1772   Terence: *Comoediae.* 4º
1772   Terence: *Comoediae.* 12º
1773   Ariosto: *Orlando Furioso.* 4 vols. 8º and 4º (see p. 122)
1773   Shaftesbury: *Characteristicks* . . . 3 vols. 8º
1773   Lucretius: *De Rerum Natura.* 12º
1773   Sallust and Florus. 4º
1773   *Fellows: *Hymns on Believers Baptism.* 12º
1774   Sallust and Florus. 12º
1774   Bowlker: *The Art of Angling* . . . 12º
1774   *Fellows: *Six Views of Believers Baptism* . . . 12º
1774   Hunter: *The Anatomy of the Human Gravid Uterus.* 1º

*These books do not have John Baskerville's name on the title page.

BIBLIOGRAPHY

Bennett   William Bennett: *John Baskerville, The Birmingham Printer, His Press, Relations and Friends.* (Birmingham. Vol. I, 1937; Vol. II, 1939)

Benton   Josiah Henry Benton: *John Baskerville, Type-Founder and Printer.* (Boston. 1914; 2nd ed. New York. 1944)

B & J   W. Turner Berry and A. F. Johnson: *Catalogue of Specimens of Printing Types.* (London. 1935)

Besterman   Theodore Besterman (ed.): *Voltaire's Correspondence.* (Geneva. v.d.)

B & W   E. C. Bigmore and C. W. H. Wyman: *A Bibliography of Printing.* (London. 1880; reprinted 1969)

Carlyle   *Autobiography of the Rev. Dr. Alexander Carlyle.* (London. 2nd ed. 1860)

Cave   Thomas Cave: *John Baskerville: The Printer 1706–1775 His Ancestry.* (Birmingham. 1936)

Chalmers   Alexander Chalmers: *The General Biographical Dictionary.* Revised and enlarged. (London. v.d.)

Derrick   Samuel Derrick: *Letters Written From Leverpoole, Chester . . .* (Dublin. 1767)

Dibdin: Library Companion   T. F. Dibdin: *The Library Companion; or, The Young Man's Guide . . .* (London. 1824)

Dibdin: Classics   Thomas Frognall Dibdin: *An Introduction to the Knowledge of Rare and Valuable Editions of the Greek and Roman Classics.* 2 vols. (London. 4th ed. 1827)

Dreyfus: The Library   John Dreyfus: *The Baskerville Punches 1750–1950* in *The Library*, Fifth Series, Vol. v, No. 1, 1950.

BIBLIOGRAPHY

Dreyfus: Signature John Dreyfus: *Baskerville's Methods of Printing* in *Signature*, new series 12. (London. 1951)

Franklin *The Papers of Benjamin Franklin.* (Yale. v.d.)

Gaskell Philip Gaskell: *John Baskerville A Bibliography.* (Cambridge. 1959; 2nd ed. 1973)

Hansard T. C. Hansard: *Typographia . . .* (London. 1825)

Hanson L. W. Hanson: *Review* and *Bibliographical Notes* in *The Library*, Fifth Series, Vol. xv, 1960.

Harwood Edward Harwood: *A View of the Various Editions of the Greek and Roman Classics . . .* (London. 4th ed. 1790)

Hill Joseph Hill: *The Book Makers of Old Birmingham . . .* (Birmingham. 1907)

Horne Thomas Hartwell Horne: *An Introduction to the Study of Bibliography . . .* (London. 1814)

Hutton W. Hutton: *An History of Birmingham to the End of the Year 1780.* (Birmingham. 1781)

Jay Leonard Jay: *Letters of the famous 18th Century Printer John Baskerville of Birmingham . . .* (Birmingham. 1932)

Kippis Andrew Kippis: *Biographica Britannica.* (London. 2nd ed. 1778)

Langford John Alfred Langford: *A Century of Birmingham Life, or A Chronicle of Local Events from 1741 to 1841.* 2 vols. (Birmingham. 1868)

M & Q Margaret L. Mare and W. H. Quarrel: *Lichtenberg's Visits to England.* (Oxford. 1938)

Mores Edward Rowe Mores: *A Dissertation upon English Typographical Founders and Founderies.* (London. 1963. Ed. Harry Carter and Christopher Ricks)

Nichols: Lit. Anec. John Nichols: *Literary Anecdotes of the Eighteenth Century.* (London. 1812 etc.)

Nichols: Illustrations John Nichols: *Illustrations of the Literary History of the Eighteenth Century.* (London. 1817 etc.)

Noble Mark Noble: *A Biographical History of England . . .* 3 vols. (London. 1806)

S & D Ralph Straus and Robert K. Dent: *John Baskerville. A Memoir.* (London. 1907)

BIBLIOGRAPHY

TBR   Talbot Baines Reed: *A History of the Old English Letter Foundries.*
(London. 1952. Ed. by A. F. Johnson)

T & C   R. D. Townsend and M. Currier: *A Selection of Baskerville
Imprints . . . in Papers in Honor of Andrew Keogh.* (New Haven. 1938)

Walker   Benjamin Walker: *The Resting Places of the Remains of John
Baskerville . . .* (Birmingham. 1944)

Williams   Marjorie Williams: *Letters of William Shenstone.* (Oxford.
1939)

INDEX

DATE DUE

JUN 0 1 1999			

DEMCO